I0106230

INDiE AUTHOR MAGAZINE

HELLO AND WELCOME!

I'm Indie Annie, and I'm thrilled you're reading this gorgeous full-color version of IAM. Did you know that you can also access all the information, education, and inspiration in our app? It's available on both the iOS App Store and Google Play. And for those that prefer to listen to me read articles, you can pop over to Spotify or our website. Happy Reading!

X

IndieAuthorMagazine.com

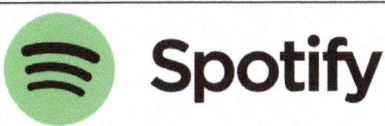

Download on the
App Store

GET IT ON
Google Play

Spotify

PAID ADS

ON THE COVER

INDIE AUTHOR MAGAZINE

PUBLISHER
Chelle Honiker

CREATIVE DIRECTOR
Alice Briggs

EDITOR IN CHIEF
Nicole Schroeder

COPY EDITOR
Lisa Thompson

WRITERS
Angela Archer
Elaine Bateman
Patricia Carr
Bradley Charbonneau
Laurel Decher
Fatima Fayez
Gill Fernley
Greg Fishbone
Chrishaun Keller-Hanna
Jac Harmon
Marion Hermannsen
Natalie Hobbs

WRITERS
Kasia Lasinska
Megan Linski-Fox
Bre Lockhart
Sìne Màiri MacDougall
Angie Martin
Merri Maywether
Susan Odev
Jenn Mitchell
Clare Sager
Nicole Schroeder
Emilia Zeeland

PUBLISHER
Athenia Creative
6820 Apus Dr.
Sparks, NV, 89436 USA
775.298.1925

ISSN 2768-7880 (online)–ISSN 2768-7872 (print)

The publication, authors, and contributors reserve their rights in regards to copyright of their work. No part of this work covered by the copyright may be reproduced or copied in any form or by any means without the written consent of the publisher. All copyrighted work was reproduced with the permission of the owner.

Reasonable care is taken to ensure that *Indie Author Magazine* articles and other information on the website are up to date and as accurate as possible, at the time of publication, but no responsibility can be taken by *Indie Author Magazine* for any errors or omissions contained herein. Furthermore, *Indie Author Magazine* takes no responsibility for any losses, damages, or distress resulting from adherence to any information made available through this publication. The opinions expressed are those of the authors and do not necessarily reflect the views of *Indie Author Magazine*.

From the Publisher

There's an old saying that goes, "If you're going through Hell—keep going. That's no place to stop."

The same can be said about first drafts, editing, and most of the business tasks associated with being a self-published author. Many of the tasks aren't in our wheelhouse as creatives, or we do them so infrequently that we lose the momentum and muscle memory that comes with repetition.

Every new year, instead of making resolutions, I choose a focus word. One year it was "health," and another it was "abundance."

I keep that word in front of me and try to make decisions in support of it the entire year.

This year, my word is "consistency."

Striving for consistency, I try to keep my practices and habits simple so I can avoid decision fatigue. Rather than a marathon writing session to hit a deadline, I try to write every morning for two hours. I know what every meal will be each week. I wear the same outfits day in and day out.

It's not easy. It gets mind-numbingly boring. But I'm trying to build a muscle so strong that it won't atrophy when I choose a new word next year.

Do I blow it? Sure. But rather than "starting over" with my diet, or my errant word count, I keep going. I don't try to catch up. I don't wait for a milestone like a Monday or the first day of the month to start again.

I keep going.

Because, dear friends, sometimes it feels like Hell.

To your success,
Chelle
Publisher
Indie Author Magazine

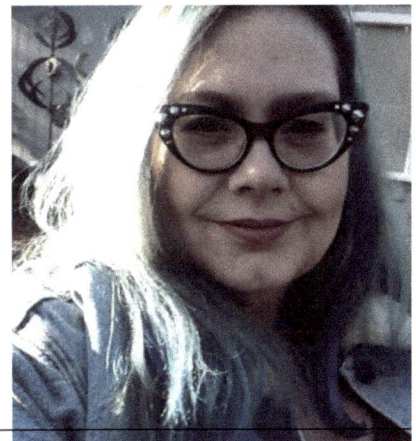

From the Editor

As indie authors, we are constantly introducing ourselves: to other writers, to editors, to cover designers, and especially—ideally—to new readers. For a profession that can sometimes feel a bit lonely, we're rarely going it alone, which makes our first impressions important … and all the more daunting.

Speaking of introductions, some of you might recognize my byline from previous issues of this magazine, but for many of you, this is your first opportunity to put a name to my words. I've been part of *Indie Author Magazine* for over a year now and an editor since December 2021, and I'm thrilled now to be assuming the role of editor in chief.

I'm still an aspiring indie; I've always had plenty of works in progress, but I've yet to cross the finish line that would put them in the hands of readers. Yet from *IAM*'s inception, there's been something special about the stories and advice shared in these pages. Even before I've fully entered the writing world, they've inspired me in my author journey, letting me daydream about reaching bestseller status or giving me ideas for my bare-bones marketing plan. I'm consistently proud of the content our writers produce, and I can't wait to share what else they have in store for you down the road.

In a way, it feels fitting to introduce, or re-introduce, myself to you in this issue. Our stories this month are all about creating connections that last. Whether you're trying to craft an eye-catching advertisement—the quintessential introduction to potential new readers—or sparking up Clubhouse conversations and work relationships with other authors, I hope they'll make those first encounters a little more enjoyable.

From there, the story is just beginning.

Nicole Schroeder
Editor-In-Chief
Indie Author Magazine

PLANNING TRAVEL TO A CONFERENCE?

Use miles.

Explore ways to make the most of your award miles.

Writelink.to/unitedair

First Things First

Everyone buys the first book in a series. When you run promotions, they'll be for the first in the series. When readers ask you where to start, it'll be with the first in the series. When you calculate the viability of a series based on read-through or buy-through, the first book is your baseline. Everything else will be a subset of that first book's numbers.

The first book can be longer than the others in the series. That's better from a revenue perspective because everyone gets the first book. If you participate in the KDP Select (Kindle Unlimited) program, then your page reads from the first book will bring home more revenue for you.

You won't have more people reading the second book in a series than read the first. Even with a ninety-nine percent read-through rate, you lose one reader out of every one hundred. Anything north of fifty percent is a good number of readers moving to the second book in the series. That means only half of the readers will pick up the second book. (But with future volumes in a series, more people will pick up the

IT ALL COMES BACK TO BOOK NUMBER ONE

first book. You see how the snowball gains mass as it rolls?) From the second to the third, you want a number of ninety percent or higher, and from the third to fourth and later books in a series, you want a consistent ninety-plus percent.

And it all comes back to the first book.

Will later books in a series be written better? Probably, but that first book is your exploration of a new idea, the development of new characters, and the world-building that adds color to the backdrop of an exciting story.

First books are written with passion and energy. Readers can tell. The authors can feel it too. Build a better springboard from which to leap higher into your author career.

Let that first book be a beacon for those that follow, a signpost to a great adventure, and most importantly, the moneymaker. Turn it loose, and let it earn its keep (even as a loss leader, which is a different topic, but if it gets readers into the series, you win).

The first book. Everyone always buys the first book. ■

Craig Martelle

PLAN YOUR BOOKS
THE WAY YOU THINK

Plottr

Outline faster, plot smarter, and turbocharge your productivity today with the #1 visual book planning software for writers.

USE CODE "IAM" FOR 10% OFF

https://writelink.to/plottr

AUTHOR·TECH·SUMMIT
Begins: August 30, 2022
AuthorTechSummit.com
Need tech to increase your productivity and profits?
Join us for free, and get to know the tools and classes that will help you keep cool in the current economic weather conditions.
Have a tool or class? Let's chat.

Dear Indie Annie,

I want to write a Fantasy series, and I love Tolkien's world-building with various cultures, geographies, and even languages. But I feel like I'm getting completely bogged down in world-building and wonder if I'm making parts of my world that aren't even important. How do I know how much world-building to do for a rich story without getting lost and not actually writing the series?

Builder in Batajnica

DEAR BUILDER,

What a lovely problem to have.

Like many authors, I love those initial stages when you are mapping out a new series and you give yourself permission to explore the landscape that your fresh, shiny new characters are going to inhabit. This discovery phase is so important. If you want to create a believable world filled with relatable characters, even if those characters are part of a vampiric subspecies with iridescent skin, it is an activity worth taking time over.

We all know there are only a handful of plotlines in reality. These same stories—boy meets girl, the hero's journey, etc.—have been passed down since the beginning of time. Every book ever written plays with and twists these tropes into something new and fresh. Often, that is achieved through placing the story in a new world. *Star Wars* is the classic Western-style tale of good versus evil set in space; *West Side Story* is a refashioning of *Romeo and Juliet*, and so on.

So setting is key. It impacts your characters and influences their actions. Star-crossed lovers in fourteenth-century Verona have the same passions and desires as 1950s Manhattan. However, Romeo and Juliet are at odds with their families; Tony and Maria, with their ethnic communities. The historical period matters as well, and both parties are impacted by the economic, political, and even racial attitudes of their time.

But Shakespeare and Bernstein/Sondheim/Laurents had the advantage of setting their stories in a historical place and time they either lived in or could research. If you are creating a fantasy world, you have to create a multilayered universe that establishes a world as rich and multifaceted as our own.

How long you should take to create this world is dependent on several factors:

- Do you have a deadline for publication?

Need help from your favorite Indie Aunt?
Ask Dear Indie Annie a question at
IndieAnnie@indieauthormagazine.com

- Are you writing a stand-alone book, a trilogy, or a series?
- Do you plan to write one or more spin-off series?
- Do you want to make any money from this venture?

The first three factors, dear Builder, I believe are self-explanatory. If you have a deadline, then you need to decide how much time you need in advance to pace yourself toward that deadline. How long do you need to edit and format? How long will it take to produce your first draft? If you know these things, then work backward from the deadline. What's left between now and the total number of weeks before the deadline countdown begins is how long you have to explore your world.

Nothing focuses your mind like a deadline.

Yes, some things you discover will be surplus to requirements, but giving yourself a deadline means that at least you will stop diving down rabbit holes and start writing sooner. Those micro-details may be useful to know later on, but you may also find that you have to create some information on the spot because, despite all your planning, you forgot to decide whether, in your world, coffee is made from java beans or some strange new concoction made with blue bat droppings.

The same rationale applies if you are planning a trilogy or series, including any spin-offs. You need to start writing at some point. So set a deadline and begin. The only difference between a stand-alone novel and a trilogy or series is that with a longer run, you will have more opportunities to use some of the details you worked on in the discovery phase. Be sure to give yourself time to enjoy the world-building phase but establish an end date because I would argue, dear friend, that the most important factor lies in your answer to my last question above.

If you want to make money, you will have to hit "Publish."

Now, of course, if you have created a vivid world that captures your readers' imaginations, like George Lucas, you can turn that world into a myriad of profitable spin-offs and merchandising opportunities. From the original idea in 1973, Lucas capitalized on a dream that has fed him well since *Star Wars* hit our screens in 1977. Bear in mind, though, that four years were spent in production, and the initial world-building took a fraction of that time.

My advice, dearest, darling Builder, is to start writing. You will soon find out if your world needs more work. Don't just paint a landscape—populate it with actors and make them busy. Test out your world, and get it in front of readers as soon as possible.

Happy writing,
Indie Annie

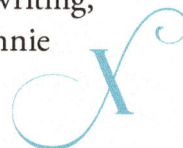

10 TIPS FOR

CANVA

Full disclosure: Canva is my friend. This user-friendly graphic design app is similar to Photoshop or Affinity. I use it for Facebook, Twitter, TikTok, Instagram, Pinterest, YouTube, and my newsletter. A free account with the site can be great for mood boards, meme-making, and book cover design. For an annual $120 subscription, Canva Pro also offers additional access to a wider library of images, more storage, a brand kit, a social media scheduler, and a calendar to keep it organized.

Most articles on the internet about the platform discuss the basics of how to use Canva. I'll address some of those tips, but I'm a "why" person. How will knowing what Canva has to offer help move my indie publishing image forward? That means sales and reader engagement after they've bought my book or signed up for my newsletter.

Like any author platform, the answer starts with helping you understand the tools you have at your disposal. I'll focus on the free version of Canva for authors who want to try out its features before spending money on a professional account. With that being said, here are our top ten tips for using Canva:

1 VISIT THE CANVA DESIGN SCHOOL

Canva has videos, blogs, and tutorials to help navigate its features. In the "Features" tab on the home screen, Canva graphic designers post short videos that take the guesswork out of using the platform. Here, an author can learn how to design graphics for websites, book covers, newsletters, merchandising, and social media engagement.

2 START WITH A DESIGN TEMPLATE

I cannot design a wheel, but I know how to add hearts and flowers to make it pretty. That also works with templates. They lay the groundwork for font sizing and image placement. The beauty of this method is once you've modified the template to suit your brand, you have a template you can duplicate and update. To give a feel for the options, Canva has over 1,800 book cover templates, 340,000 Instagram templates, 150,000 Facebook templates, and 5,000 Twitter templates, as well as numerous templates for websites, infographics, recipe books, and email headers. With a Canva Pro account, you can resize the template for a specific platform, such as adjusting a post for Instagram to also work on Twitter.

3 USE THE RULER AND GRID LINES

This handy feature is under the "File" tab. When these features are chosen, lines appear whenever an image or text moves. It has crosshairs for the middle of the graphic and lines that make it easier to line up text and images. This nifty tool can mean fewer instances of downloading an image to discover that it is off-center, only to have to go back and fix it. Rulers and grid lines save time—and therefore sanity.

4 USE THE COLOR MATCH TOOL

Once you've chosen images, Canva will show you the colors within the image that would work. Scroll down to the bottom of the color tab to view and select specific colors. This takes the guesswork out of what to use for compliments and contrasts. For users who have Canva Pro, it will also post your brand colors, making it easier to maintain brand uniformity.

5 CONNECT CANVA WITH YOUR FAVORITE APPS

Use the "Discover Apps" option to post directly from Canva to Facebook, Instagram, and Pinterest. Canva connects with Tenor GIF and Google Maps, making it easy for users to import images for their designs. In the "Favorite Apps" section, Canva highlights updates to what they offer. The newest additions are smart mockups, flipbooks, and integration with communication channels like Slack and Mailchimp.

6 ADD YOUR BRAND'S FONTS TO THE LIBRARY

Canva has hundreds of fonts. But if the font for your brand isn't in there, you can add it to the font library. When searching for a font, scroll to the bottom. There, you'll see the "Upload a Font" option. Now you can make graphics with fonts specific to your branding.

7 SHARE LINKS TO YOUR DESIGNS

Canva has a "view only" link. If you have something in the works and want to share updates with your followers, share the link to your project. If you want to take it a step further, you can share a link so that others can comment on your work. Followers then have the opportunity for additional engagement and feel as if they were there from the beginning.

Pro Tip: Add the link to your newsletter or to your Patreon feed. The "view only" feature would emphasize to these readers that they are your superfans and privy to your art first.

8 BUY MERCHANDISE

One time, I made myself a cute coffee cup with my logo. I bought one cup, thinking nobody would want a mug with my name on it. Holding the cup, I shared a "good morning" picture with my group. Color me surprised. The gals in my group wanted a cup with my name on it. Now when I want to give my readers some author love, I can order cups, stickers, T-shirts, hoodies, bookmarks, notebooks, calendars, and tote bags directly from Canva.

9 SEARCH FOR ENGAGEMENT IDEAS

Learn from my mistakes. I once spent a good chunk of time designing an engagement bingo game. The idea was great, people shared it on Facebook, and my following grew. It was worth the effort, but I later learned that my work could have been reduced significantly. Canva offers the ability for users to create similar engagement ideas in only a few minutes' time. Type "engagement" in the search bar. You'll find loads of ideas for various ways to promote engagement with your followers. There are "this or that" posts, bingo posts, "would you rather" posts, and more already created that you can modify to match your brand.

10 ORGANIZE YOUR MATERIALS INTO FOLDERS

If you frequent Canva for simple designs and artwork, the images you've created can accumulate after a while. Luckily, the site allows you to sort images into folders to make finding old designs easier. Keep projects in files that can be organized by book titles, series, seasons, types of engagement—you get the idea. This way, you can easily access your images for use in the years to come.

Pro Tip: Make a folder and stack folders within. For example, start with your series; within the series, make a folder for each title. Another way to keep things organized is to have an engagement folder. Within the engagement folder, have a file for holidays, page takeovers, bookish engagement, and promo engagement.

Canva is an app that takes the guesswork out of designing images that help authors connect with readers. These are the top ten tips we've accumulated, but you can also explore other useful corners of the platform. Visit the site, use the tabs, and make friends with the search bar. Then have fun making images that will wow your readers. ■

Merri Maywether

Accidentally Manifesting the Dream

FROM SAN DIEGO TO SCOTLAND, TAMERI ETHERTON DAZZLES READERS WITH HER SELF-MADE AUTHOR CAREER

Tameri Etherton discovered she was a natural storyteller when she was six.

"I have three older siblings and then a stepsister who was four months younger than me, and we'd go camping a lot," she says. "And I would be the one telling stories around the fire. And I realized I had a gift for storytelling, and it entertained people and it made them feel things."

Like many writers, the discovery that her words moved readers emotionally was a heavy hit of dopamine, and little Tameri was hooked. The transition from family storyteller to writer came later.

"In high school, I had an honors English teacher who was like, 'You need to do something with this,'" she says. "And she really made me feel for the first time that I could do it, that I was a good writer."

Tameri and I are chatting via Zoom on a Saturday afternoon. I'm in Texas, and she's in Edinburgh, Scotland. Full disclosure—she and I have been in an online group for the better part of a year: part book club, part writing technique dissection and discussion. We met at 2019's 20BooksTo50K® conference in Edinburgh, so this is less a formal interview and more a chat with a friend who fascinates and inspires me with her work ethic and inquisitive passion for perfecting her craft. I've come to know her as someone who asks thoughtful questions and gives and receives criticism generously, which is one reason we both agree her career as a full-time indie author has taken off.

Her career has led her and husband, Dave, around the world, from their native sunny San Diego to now beloved Scotland. They relocated permanently in 2015 with the blessing of their adult children. She says she accidentally manifested this after visiting several times over the course of a decade with the kids while Dave was working. When Dave's company had an opening, he asked her how long he should commit to working in Scotland, thinking it would be temporary and they would go back and forth between the United States and the United Kingdom.

"Should I just tell him nine months? Tell 'em nine years. I was manifesting it without even realizing I was manifesting it."

Temporary became permanent when they bought their central Edinburgh home less than a year later. After looking at hundreds of places to fulfill her "princess demands," Tameri says, the couple found one that ticked all the boxes with a view of the castle and within walking distance of Dave's work.

LADY DAZZLETON HAS ENTERED THE CHAT

We mustn't forget the real subject of this interview: a pink stuffed dragon named Lady Dazzleton currently perched awkwardly on Tameri's shoulder, her constant companion on adventures around Scotland and points beyond. You'll see "Lady D" more than Tameri and Dave in photos on her social media account, as the fabulous dragon serves as both avatar and alter ego.

"I had a fabulous web goddess … who made my logo, and it's a little teacup with a dragon on it," Tameri says. "We called her 'Lady,' and she was pink and sparkly. And then one day, I found Lady Dazzleton."

Lady Dazzleton will have her own series eventually, but for now, she's an outlet—and part-time scapegoat—for mischief.

"She's a hard-drinking, hard-loving, leave-him-in-the-morning dragon," Tameri quips. "Her book will be titled *The Mis-Adventures of Lady D*."

Since Lady D is the instigator of shenanigans, I ask if she's the one to carry the bail money in case one of their adventures goes south, and with a laugh, she tells me the money stays with humans. Even though Lady D could technically fly out of her hypothetical jail cell, she says, she would stick around to hear the stories so she could relay them to Tameri later to write down.

FINDING HER OWN VOICE

Tameri's first novel was written without the help of her incident-causing friend. After graduating from college with a degree in literature and writing, she planned to go into teaching after one of her professors discouraged her from writing what she loved to read, which he referred to as genre fiction. Tameri says he meant that as an insult.

Tameri put any idea of writing professionally away and focused on raising her two young children. But the seed of blending Romance and Fantasy was already planted.

"My mother is a voracious Romance reader," she says. "She could have opened a used bookstore with all of her books. She had, I think [at] last count, six thousand. And so I grew up reading Romance, and then I went into Fantasy."

She was a frequent volunteer at her children's schools. When her youngest started third grade at a new school, Tameri was told they didn't have volunteers. She struggled with a two-month depression because of the change.

"I seriously did not know who I was because I had put my entire soul into raising these two little humans for fifteen years."

Her husband asked, "Why don't you write that book that you always talk about?"

Seven years later, she found herself still grappling with finishing the story, making the mistake of going to general critique groups and not Fantasy-loving critique groups. Every week, they had her rewrite Chapter One, which she did some forty times before finally deciding to push through a different way. She hired a developmental editor in 2012, joined Romance Writers of America, and started learning about self-publishing.

"At the time, traditional publishing was the thing everybody had to do to be legitimate. And then there are people like Bella Andre and Marie Force, and they actually came, and they spoke at RWA San Diego. And I heard how you could make this happen, and you don't need [traditional] publishers."

She calls that first book "the book of my heart" but admits she still had a lot to learn to make it commercially viable. The cover was "old school" and mimicked writers she loved, but it didn't match readers' expectations. She changed the cover and the title when she received feedback that it "didn't mean anything" to them.

Learning and adapting has become a pillar of her career, and she notes some things she learned ten years ago weren't lessons she was

> "At the end of the day, it's a product," she says. "It's not my baby. It was my baby when I was writing it, but the minute I published it, it belonged to the readers."

ready for. Now she'll reread a book and the concepts make total sense, but she's careful not to embrace every new idea.

She says the biggest lessons she's learned have been to be adaptable, to be ready to pivot, and to not consider anything she writes too precious. "At the end of the day, it's a product," she says. "It's not my baby. It was my baby when I was writing it, but the minute I published it, it belonged to the readers."

Despite the book belonging to the readers, she refuses to write by committee, preferring to first have five or six readers read through the first draft with instructions to give her "the harshest criticism" they can. She then takes that criticism and wades through changes she's prepared to make to her story.

THE BENEFITS OF CONFERENCES

Tameri is a confirmed extrovert, and the isolation during the pandemic was especially hard. Conferences are a welcome return, and she attended three in June. Just being with people, she says, recharges her and has done a lot to combat the depression and burnout she's experienced.

On the business side, she finds the benefits of connecting with other authors priceless.

"I can't write fast enough for just my readers," she says. "I want my readers to be your readers too. Something I love so much is when I go to these conferences, finding other authors that I can introduce to my readers."

ON SUCCESS AND FUTURE PLANS

When asked what's next for her career, she quickly replies, "I have world domination in my planner," admitting that she'll need to work up to that. She likes Joanna Penn's philosophy of being "quietly successful" and living her best life without the trappings of fame.

Her motivation remains clear: She wants to continue to entertain and tell stories.

"The beautiful thing about this gig is that we don't have to stop. We can keep writing until we just stop and keel over," she says.

It goes without saying that if that happens, Lady Dazzleton's alibi should be verified by the authorities. ■

Chelle Honiker

Breaking Bread (and Churros) across Europe: 20Books Madrid in Review

There is no substitute for in-person events. "You'll learn a few things from the books, you'll get quite a bit from the professors, but where the real knowledge and experience comes from, what you really need to make an effort to focus on, are your classmates." That was the advice I received from a graduating student as I started my two-year MBA degree. Dare ask me which of those three things I value most all these years later? Well, I recently co-wrote a children's book with one of those classmates along with his kids and my own, and I talked to him just yesterday.

20Books Madrid is now in the record books, and I could categorize the event along the same lines as my MBA:

1. **Presentations (the "books"):** If you're an active indie author, chances are that you've read the books, watched the videos, and "learned all the things." That said, ideally these presentations are cutting edge with the latest and greatest information, so even if you think you know the basics, it's always great to hear it—especially live from a real person in front of you.

2. **Speakers (the "professors"):** We truly have access to the speakers, especially at a smaller conference, such as Madrid. Everyone was encouraged everyone to go up to a speaker and ask your question or just say hi. This,

of course, is the biggest benefit of coming to a conference as compared to reading the speakers' books, listening to them on a podcast, or watching them on YouTube. All of the presenters were available to chat with during the breaks. This is definitely a highlight of a smaller conference and one authors can—and should—take advantage of.

3. **Authors (the "classmates"):** Whereas the speakers might seem distant because they are so far ahead in income, number of books, experience, or all of the above, the other authors at the conference can be an even more resourceful group to connect with as they are more likely to be at or near your level. Everyone there is in the same boat and has something to share and usually something you can learn from. This is truly the most powerful reason to come to a conference, and especially one with just a few hundred people in attendance. You will have the time and the opportunity to make those connections with questions like, "How can we get our audiobook listeners to use the BookFunnel app so they'll be more receptive to our books on that platform?" or "Have you had the churros with the little bowl of dark chocolate? We're going tomorrow afternoon to get more."

So after all that, which piece of information stands out the most?

The chocolate and the churros, obviously!

Downtown Madrid boasts a café that serves up churros—and pretty much only churros. You go to one counter to place your order. The staff is decked out in white-collared shirts, there's an old-school cash register, and they give you your paper receipt and send you away.

You go stand in another line around the corner and await another waiter to seat you. Once a spot opens up in the shade outside, you are taken to your seats and he takes your order. Soon thereafter, yet another waiter delivers the only thing on the menu: a plate of hot churros and a cup of warm, gooey dark chocolate.

You break apart the long, donut-like stick, dip the end into the chocolate, and twirl it deep. The warm oil seeps onto your fingers, and soon, the churro is in your mouth, an explosion of rich chocolate, cinnamon, sugar, and delightful dough.

Share with fellow authors. Repeat.

Craig Martelle, the founder of 20BooksTo50K® and organizer, emcee, and fearless leader of the show, made it a point to say that the breaks in between the forty-five-minute presentations would be thirty minutes.

This was the core of what we authors were "supposed" to focus on: the other authors, authors just like us. Sure, we'd learn something from the presentations and the speakers, but most of the interaction, the communication, and the connection came through meeting other authors. And that was exactly the case at this year's 20Books Madrid.

KEY TAKEAWAYS FROM MADRID

As much as I want to talk about the churros and the chocolate or the intense exchanges with Kate Pickford, who invited authors up on stage to work through the main points of their story in real time in front of the entire audi-ence, here are a few high-level takeaways from the conference:

1. **Mindset:** If a guy who sits on his boat and plays with Amazon ads for an hour a day and writes two books per year can do it, so can we.

2. **A rising tide lifts all boats:** This is the 20BooksTo50K® motto, and it's especially true at an in-person event. We all help each other. We're collaborators, not competitors. Go talk to someone!

3. **Bring them in:** We need to do the work to bring the readers in. With the exception of TikTok, this includes tactics, such as ads, newsletters, and writing more books.

4. **Keep them happy:** Once you have the reader, take care of them, keep them happy, and give them more.

5. **Long game:** Like most overnight success stories, years of hard work, passion, and patience usually frame the background. Give yourself room to breathe—and live.

6. **Relationships:** Several speakers, as well as authors in the audience, talked about how they work with people they met at these conferences.

7. **Just say hi:** To create those relationships, just say hi to people. The worst that could happen is you two don't hit it off and both walk away to see if there are any more ham sandwiches. No harm, no foul. One of the best things that can happen is churros in downtown Madrid.

Maybe the biggest takeaway is what you *don't* take away. There's a firehose of information over the course of a conference, and there's no way anyone can take it all in—much less take action on all of it.

Cherry-pick a few action items and possibly some ideas on a higher-level strategy, and then execute those actions.

BONUS CONFERENCE WRAP-UP: 20BOOKS HOLLAND

The Pirates Have Landed

In between the 20Books Madrid and the Self Publishing Show Live London conferences, there was a quieter, smaller, yet possibly more disruptive conference: 20Books Holland.

The Netherlands is several years behind the United States in the indie publishing world. Authors might be frustrated when working in an environment where traditional publishing still has most of the respect of the reading public.

However, one might also see it as a new frontier. In fact, Michael Anderle, co-founder of 20BooksTo50K®, proclaimed that the indie author movement was like a pirate, the conference was the pirate ship, and independent authors have landed on the mainland.

Here are a few of the topics covered over the course of the day, all translated from Dutch as the entire day—with the exception of presentations by Craig Martelle, Michael Anderle, and Dan Wood from Draft2Digital—was in Dutch:

- Marketing and promotion panel: a hybrid publisher, a book coach, and an author talked marketing strategies and tactics
- Book trailers
- Children's books and crowdfunding
- Mailing lists and selling direct (paperbacks)

Although the country and even the region, including Belgium and Luxembourg, are lagging in the industry, it has to begin somewhere. One might say that it began at this conference.

The indies have landed! There's a bounty to be had and treasures to be discovered! Disembark and rush the beaches!

It might be a slow invasion, but it has begun. Keep an eye on indie author activities in the Netherlands. ■

Bradley Charbonneau

Design like a Pro for free

👑 Try Canva Pro today

https://writelink.to/canva

Advertising as an Indie Author

WHERE TO START

You've written your first book, revised and edited it, and finally hit that "Publish" button. You're over the moon that you've gotten your first piece out there but confused about why you're not getting the feedback you thought you would. What do you do now?

Advertising can seem intimidating, scary, and expensive for those who are just starting. Luckily, many websites and social platforms help indie authors get their books in front of the right audience.

BOOKBUB

Created in 2012, BookBub is an online platform for authors to advertise their books and get their names out there. The site has become known as one of the top ones to discover new books and new authors. All books are either free or posted at a low, discounted price. They are carefully picked by the site's editorial team, and only about 20 percent of books are published on the site. Along with finding new books and authors, BookBub has book recommendations, updates from the authors, and different articles. So why advertise your book on BookBub?

BookBub's advertisements are based on an auction system, and prices for ads on the site are always changing. Auctions work based on how much you bid for your advertisement. The winner will not end up paying what they bid for the ad; rather, they'll pay just above what the next-highest bidder pays. The auction helps advertisers create a methodical ad, arranged to help the advertiser feel most successful about their advertisement so that they can reach the correct target audience. Before entering the auction, BookBub says authors need to do four things:

1. Set a budget for their campaigns
2. Set a cost-per-click or cost-per-mille bid for their campaigns
3. Set a target
4. Edit their campaigns based on performance

BookBub posts books from the auction winners.

Once you have all of these lessons completed, you'll be entered into the auction. Once the auction is over, usually around 20 percent of the participants are chosen. If you are chosen, you will be able to advertise your book on BookBub's monthly email, but if you're not chosen, you can still do many things on the site as an author.

Based out of southern Pennsylvania, Ariele Sieling is a full-time Science Fiction and Fantasy author. Sieling says she has used BookBub in the past to advertise her books and get in front of new readers.

"The thing I like about BookBub is that they have author profiles, so readers can follow you. So every time I publish a book now, all of the people who follow me on BookBub get an email that I have a new book out," Sieling says.

Setting up a BookBub author account and gaining followers will help you reach a larger audience, and more readers will be alerted of your new releases and deals.

GOODREADS

Goodreads is an online platform that helps readers locate the best books for them. As stated on its website, its mission is to help people find and share the books they love. Even though this site is reader-based, Goodreads offers great tools for authors to promote their books. The author program on the site is free, and authors are allowed to join from anywhere. The author program allows authors to create a profile, and through that profile, authors can promote their books by running giveaways, tell their followers about upcoming releases and news, and engage with their readers. Another great aspect of the author profile system on Goodreads is the verification step. Authors can become verified on the site and receive a "Goodreads badge." Once you receive the badge, you can use the badge to tell your fans to follow you.

The website has a list of all of the benefits that come with creating your author page, including

- managing your own profile
- promoting your published and soon-to-be-published books
- interacting with your readers

TIKTOK

TikTok has quickly become one of the world's most popular social media platforms. BookTok is a sub-community of the platform that's focused on books and literature. Authors will give sneak peeks of their books, act out different skits, and even go live with their readers. TikTok is completely free for anyone to join and gives anyone a chance to be seen through their "For You Page." The "For You Page" works through an algorithm in which the app will select videos they believe fit your niche and interests, reflecting what you would want to see.

Diana Miller, an author under the pen name Raven Storm, says TikTok is her biggest platform for advertising her books right now.

"I have about fifteen thousand followers on TikTok, and I do a lot of skit videos for my books. I do skits where I pretend I'm the characters, and it gets a lot of traction for my books," Miller says.

Although TikTok is a free platform for anyone to use, there is a way for you to shine a light on your videos through paid advertising. To start advertising on TikTok, you have to turn your account into a business account, set your budget, and start posting sponsored content. TikTok ads start at ten dollars per cost-per-thousand and can range between fifty thousand dollars and one hundred twenty thousand dollars, depending on the format of the advertisement.

According to the TikTok website, 52 percent of users say they find new products on TikTok ads, and 61 percent feel as if advertise-

Miller advertising through her TikTok account

ments on TikTok are more unique than other top platforms.

TikTok lists some perks that come with advertising through the platform:

- Boost return on investment by reaching an applicable audience
- Reach new audiences in more than twenty markets
- Fast setup for every level of skill
- Pliable budget that works for different business sizes

FACEBOOK

Facebook is the most commonly used social media platform around the world, so why wouldn't you want to advertise your book there? Creating an author page on Facebook has many benefits for you and your readers. It's an easy way to communicate with your readers. An author page makes it easy to announce upcoming book releases or events you may be hosting for your book release.

Creating an author page on Facebook is fairly easy as well. All you need to do is create a Facebook account and change the account settings to become a business account. Once you have done this, you can personalize your page and start promoting your book for free.

This connection with your readers is very important. A Facebook author page is an excellent way to communicate with your readers. You can connect with them by sharing updates on books, going live and interacting with viewers, commenting back on posts in your feed, and in other ways.

Facebook also allows you to advertise on the platform with basic ads.

According to the Meta website, there are seven steps to running an advertisement on Facebook:

1. Choose your objective
2. Select your audience
3. Decide where to run your ad
4. Set your budget
5. Pick a format
6. Place your order
7. Measure and manage your ad

Once your advertisement on Facebook has been posted, you have free range to edit your campaign and track its performance.

Advertising does not have to be scary or expensive. Most platforms will allow you to pick your budget for placing ads or even be completely free. Finding a platform that allows you to engage with your audience and be creative with your advertisements will help drive traffic to your book. ■

Natalie Hobbs

Nominate a Featured Author!

Know someone making waves in the industry? Tell us about them.

How to Hook Readers with Better Ad Copy

How many ads do we see a day? The answer is hard to calculate, but according to Forbes Magazine (https://forbes.com), studies suggest we see anywhere between four thousand and ten thousand ads per day. That's not far-fetched. Back in 2015, a marketer by the name of Ron Marshall (https://redcrowmarketing.com) set out to test the stats by spending twenty-four hours counting all the ads he saw. He gave up after counting 487 ads before breakfast.

We've developed what's known as "ad blindness," so many of these exposures don't even register. So when you're the one doing the marketing, how do you catch the attention of readers with your ads?

You could go to the Facebook ads library and imitate what other authors are doing, such as putting excerpts in the body copy or leading with a review quote, but understanding key advertising concepts will stand you in far better stead.

Generally, there are five elements to an ad:

1. The ad image
2. The headline and subheading
3. The hook or preview text
4. The body copy
5. The call to action (CTA)

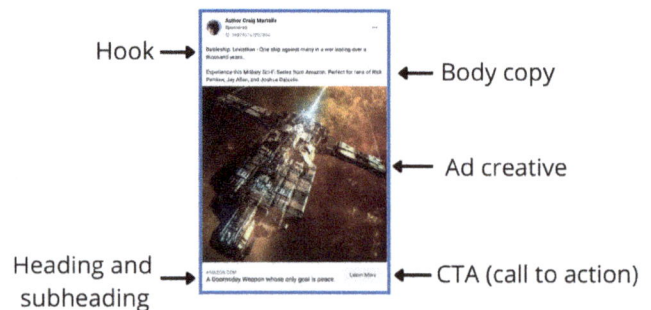

Each has its job to do. The ad image is given the largest amount of space to grab the reader's attention and stop them from scrolling away before they read the ad copy.

Because we're trained to scroll and the image moves upward, typically the next part of the ad to catch the reader's attention is the headline and subheading. These get the reader to read the next line of the copy—the hook and the body copy.

BookBub only gives you a small square of ad real estate—a 300×250-pixel image that includes your ad copy—whereas Facebook gives you more wiggle room in terms of the length of the body copy. Headlines in Facebook ads can be up to forty characters, a link description or subhead text can be up to thirty characters, and the hook or primary text can be 125 characters before the reader has to click "read more."

The same basic marketing concepts still apply with shorter ad opportunities, meaning they require just as much care and attention to detail as longer ads. In a BookBub ad, for example, there's no room for lengthy body copy, so the headline and subheading form the hook.

But let's take a closer look at the actual copy. Your first job is to understand the target audience for the ad. Just as you might speak differently on a first date compared with how you'd speak to a long-time friend, so too should you adjust your ad copy for different audiences.

The technical term for this is "market awareness." This speaks to how familiar the readers are with you and your books. If you're targeting people who are already familiar with your previous books, try to reel them in by focusing on your offer. This could mean crafting hooks based on novelty, such as a new book; scarcity, such as a limited edition; or price. However, if you're targeting readers who've never heard of you, then building trust by providing insight from other readers—called social proof—could prove a more effective hook.

WHAT ARE HOOKS, AND HOW DO YOU USE THEM?

Think of a hook like an overarching theme of a book, such as honesty, trust, or injustice; everything you write is filtered through that lens. Hooks are a similar concept in that they're the big, curiosity-provoking ideas that frame the copy, keep readers reading, and lead them further along in the buying journey. It's important to remember that it's not the job of your ad to sell the book—it only has to sell the click to get them a step closer to purchasing it.

Often, advertisers will use more than one hook. They aren't mutually exclusive, so you can layer them to really grab attention. Let's run through several hooks authors commonly use in their advertising and how you can use them too.

SOCIAL PROOF HOOKS

Social proof is essentially about building trust and credibility. We tend to look to our peers to see what they're doing and use that as a kind of barometer for our own thoughts and behavior, so if potential readers see that other people trust you, then they are more likely to do so as well.

There are several different types of social proof. Book reviews and review quotes are some of the easiest and most obvious. However, including numbers in ad copy is another solid way to hook attention. Your ad could cite the number of Kindle Unlimited downloads your book has received, or if you're reviving an old book from your backlist, you could give the total number of reviews people left.

If you're going to use reviews in your ad copy, always look for specificity. For example, "a lovely, heartwarming insight into the life of an 'ordinary' woman" is a much better review quote than just "a wonderful read."

COMPARISON HOOKS

Comparison hooks in advertising tend to focus on highlighting differences, according to Simplilearn, an online course provider. However, they are also useful if you are a newer author or trying to tap into a new audience because they allow you to leverage the familiarity of a more well-known author. Highlight similarities between your work and another author's with phrasing such as "If you like …, then you'll love …" or "This book has all the fun of X and all the danger of Y" to entice potential readers to your work—just make sure your target audience is familiar with the comparison author you choose.

EMOTIONAL HOOKS

Although much of what you're aiming for should evoke a sense of curiosity, that alone may not be enough. All great advertising should contain some element of an emotional hook, but not all emotions are created equal in advertising terms. The most potent emotions create an arousal response. Excitement and anger are more physically arousing than sadness, so use excerpts from emotional scenes that lead to curiosity, and you'll be on your way to a winning ad.

NOVELTY HOOKS

Humans crave novelty, and your new book is the ticket to creating a curiosity gap that warrants further investigation. To use this hook effectively, you need to consider your target audience. People who've already read and liked your previous work will need less convincing than those who've never heard of you before—in which case, you'll need to layer in a few more hooks to get them to want to fill the curiosity gap and click your link.

DEMONSTRATION HOOKS

We see demonstration hooks in use all the time, though we might not realize it. Ikea sets up showrooms to demonstrate how you can style a room with their products. Back in 2010, Blendtec used the demonstration hook in a series of YouTube videos called "Will it blend?" (https://youtube.com/willitblend), which has more than 292 million views to date.

Nick Kolenda explains in his book, *Imagine Reading This*, that before we make a decision, we imagine the outcome. Video marketing enables us to create more vivid mental pictures compared with text alone, and when people can see a product in use, they are better able to imagine themselves using it—or in the case of books, reading it. If you've ever wondered, this is one reason TikTok page flips are effective when selling books.

Remember that people aren't scrolling through social media looking to buy your book. In order to interrupt their day, you need to try and enter the conversation in their minds.

Although it would be lovely to set an ad and forget it so we can focus on writing the next book, sadly, we can't. Ads are a constant work in progress. They fatigue—thanks, novelty hook. But by having a grasp on the various hooks you can use in your ad copy and understanding your target audience, you can always come up with new angles and new ad copy to test. ◼

Angela Archer

ADVERTISING 3

Finding Mr. Write

YOUR GUIDE TO CHOOSING THE PERFECT CO-WRITING PARTNER

Writing a book with another author can be like getting married. You have to settle multiple legalities and sign contracts before the writing even begins. Because this decision is so important, you must choose the right partner. Pairing up to complete a project with someone who's an ill fit can prove to be more than a headache; it can be detrimental to an author's career. On the flip side, a valuable partner can *make* an author's career with a co-writing project launching both into massive success.

The decision to co-write is far from one to take lightly. This guide will enable you to make the right decision.

ARE YOU SEARCHING IN THE RIGHT PLACES?

Finding a co-author isn't as simple as posting a notice in an online forum and hoping for a response. It can be, but the

best co-writing relationships are established when people have an existing relationship, preferably in person, before deciding to work together. You should get to know the person you want to work with for at least a year so you can see how they handle a variety of publishing challenges. Writing conventions, author get-togethers, and writing retreats can be a great way to meet other writers face-to-face and observe their business strategies before you decide to take the plunge.

DO YOU HAVE SIMILAR WRITING STYLES?

It's not enough for you and your co-author to write in the same genre. Your writing styles must be similar. Both of you must have the same idea as to where the story is going and use a similar tone of voice so as to give the reader a seamless experience as they move through the story. Similarities in craft are vital as the book you're working on together must feel like one fluid product rather than two competing ideas. Even if you and the co-author choose to write two different perspectives in two different characters, these perspectives must be read as one clear idea.

DO YOU HAVE COMPLEMENTARY PERSONALITIES?

Your personality should complement your co-writer's. The two of you should have similar opinions on writing and the industry as a whole, as well as a dynamic with each other that benefits readers. This dynamic should present an ebb and flow of ideas and responsibilities that both of you share. When one of you is struggling to fulfill your duties as a co-writer, the other should overcompensate until, eventually, the positions switch. Not everyone can be at their best all the time, and it's important to lean on each other for support.

At the same time, your relationship with your co-writer should round out each other's strengths and weaknesses. One person should focus on the big picture of the story and marketing while the other should pay attention to the small details in both. If you have editing experience, your co-author should have marketing expertise. If you enjoy administrative work but hate proofing audiobooks, you can take on the back end of the necessary admin duties while your co-author produces the audiobooks. Whatever weaknesses you have, your co-author should be able to make up for them with their own experiences and vice versa.

Choose someone based on their compatibility with you and your writing style, not what they can do for your career. Agreeing to write with a popular or big-name author can sound exciting at first, but if the partnership is not the right match, the chances of you obtaining success and being happy with the finished product are actually less than they would be if you'd chosen a lesser-known individual who's willing to work hard and compromise on ideas.

DO YOU BOTH HAVE A BUSINESS MINDSET?

Co-authors need to be committed to the task and the project at hand. It is imperative that the co-writer you choose be intent on seeing the project through, regardless of how the book is performing or how difficult the writing process becomes. Troughs in sales and hard times must be endured together. Co-writing is a long-term relationship, and it takes creativity, imagination, and grit to come up with solutions to obstacles together.

There is no room for stubbornness in co-writing. You must compromise and come to an agreement on what both of you want, which is ultimately what's best for the project. This might not be what's best for you personally. Because of this, both parties need to be team players. You need to co-write with someone who can thoughtfully contemplate feedback without getting offended by any changes or pivots you might need to make—and in co-writing, there are a lot of them.

In co-writing, every decision is a team decision, and working together is the only way to come to a productive outcome. The best co-writing teams are made of individuals who have a mutual respect for each other. These writers are willing to work together through good times and bad in order to achieve their united goal. Your future co-author should be willing to do the same, no matter what trials or rewards you may face. Your teamwork as authors will carry you exponentially further than you could've gone on your own. ■

Megan Linski-Fox

One Service to Rule Them All

AUTHOR HELPER SUITE GIVES USERS A HAND WITH ORGANIZING THE BACKEND OF BOOK BUSINESSES

Although it might sound like a bit of a stretch, "one service to rule them all" comes directly from a testimonial blurb about Author Helper Suite (AHS) from bestselling author Shane Silvers. Endorsements from big names like Silvers are a boon for any subscription tool, but any author who has used AHS will attest to the fact that it lives up to the hype.

With the ability to manage everything from reader teams to promotion tracking to custom link creation, plus more than two dozen analytic tools, this platform is a must-have for growing and managing your author business. When creating AHS in 2017, indie authors John Logsdon and Ben Zackheim tapped into their information technology background and passion for helping their fellow authors. What they came away with was a well-designed tool set that covers all the usual bases and many more.

WHAT DOES AHS OFFER?

According to its website, "The Author Helper Suite is made up of four main features that provide authors with a comprehensive toolset to launch and market books":

1. AuthorAnalytics: tracks sales, read-through, sell-through, return on investment (ROI), and ad click-through rate (CTR) and provides historical reports
2. AuthorPlanner: tracks essential marketing tasks for launches and promotions
3. ReaderTeams: allows you to work with your reader team to track manuscript issues and team participation
4. ReaderLinks: creates geo-links, affiliate support links, QR Codes, custom links, and your own MyBooks Page

On the surface, this may look like just a list of standard features, but what makes AHS stand out among its competitors is the amount of additional functionality added within them. As of June 2022, AHS offers twenty-five tools with plans to offer even more in the future.

The website is laid out in an intuitive dashboard format with each of the major features accessible from easy-to-find tabs across the top.

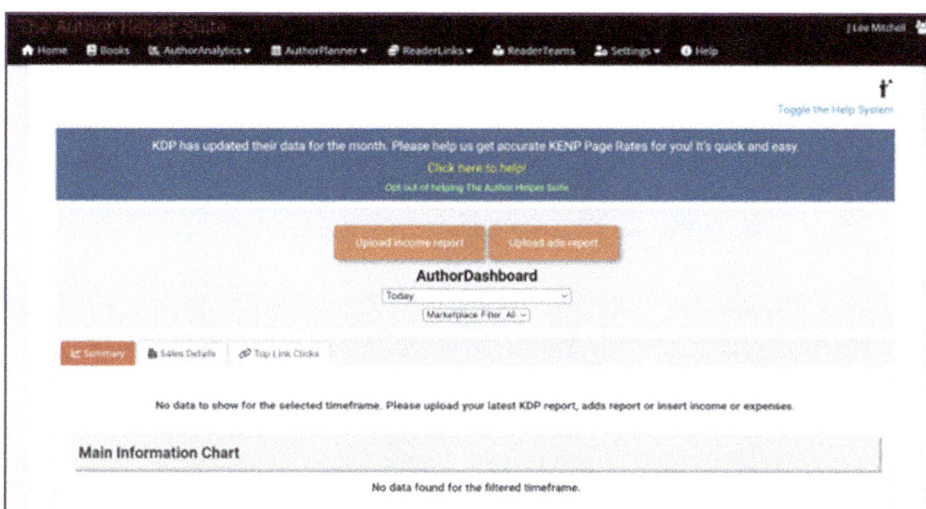

The AHS Author Dashboard tabs are located across the top of the screen.

AUTHORANALYTICS

Starting with the AuthorAnalytics feature, tools like Sell-Thru/Read-Thru for series analysis or customizable income and expense tracking could be a real game changer for authors seeking a platform that provides meaningful insights into sales and ad metrics.

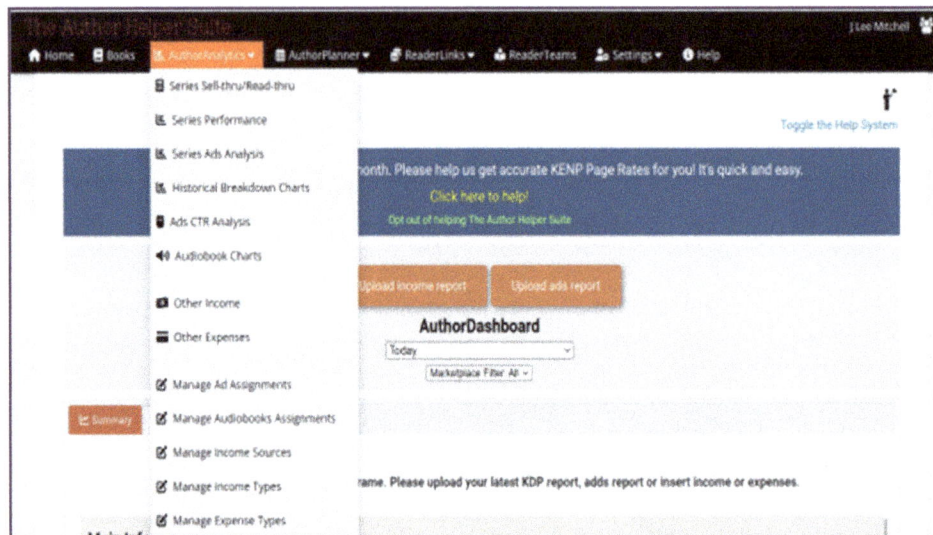

The AuthorAnalytics dropdown list contains the tracking and analytic tools.

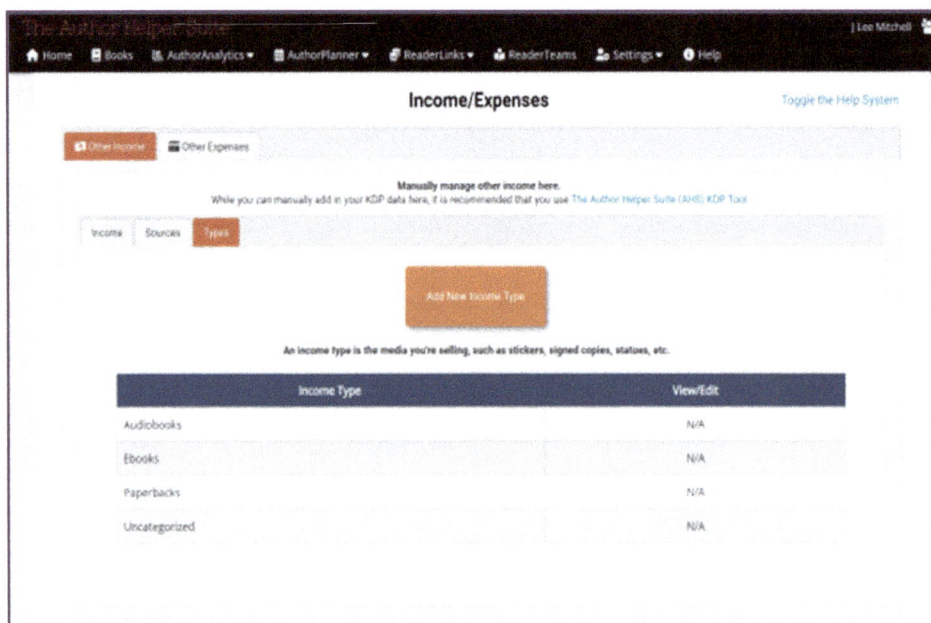

Drill down through AuthorAnalytics to Manage Income Type to apply customization.

AUTHORPLANNER

The AuthorPlanner tab features a calendar for tracking and viewing all your important tasks and promotions. One of the unique features available with this tool is the ability to not just display promotions on your calendar but also to rate and record promo performance data within the promotion entry itself.

The AuthorPlanner drop-down list provides access to planning tools.

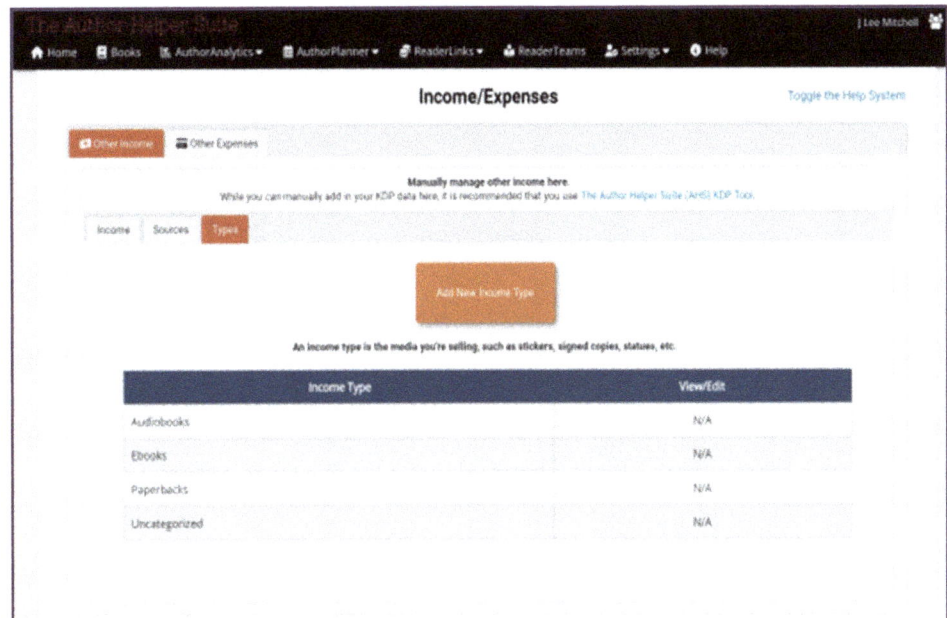

READERTEAMS

The ReaderTeams tab is the gateway to one of the most robust features AHS has to offer. The functionality found within this tab provides authors with the ability to manage all aspects of their reader teams. Reader teams can be set up and managed at an individual book or series level, and essential information, such as participation terms, announcements, questions for readers, and requests for reviews can be customized as needed. Additional tabs allow you to view open and closed issues reported by your readers.

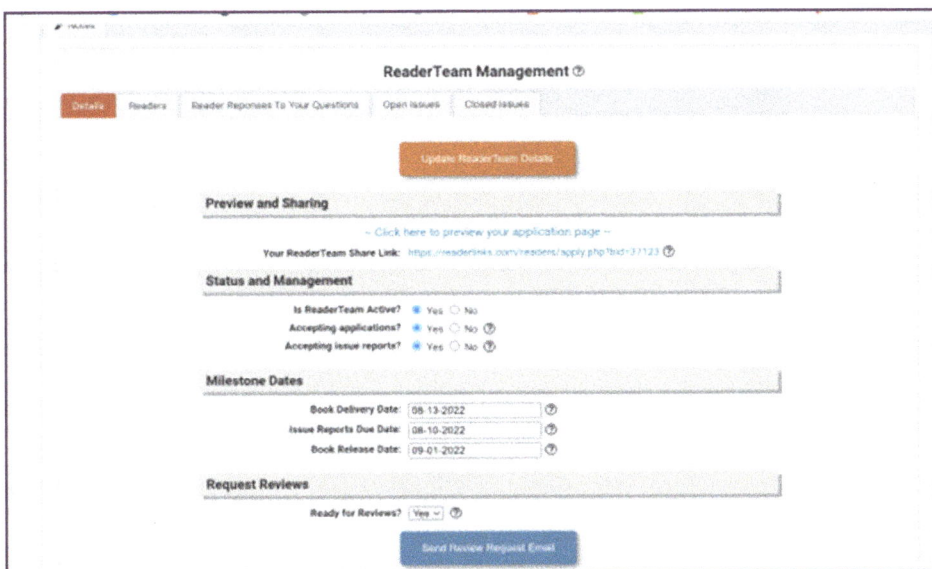

The ReaderTeam Management Interface allows users to set up and manage their reader teams.

Once you've completed the Details tab, a landing page is created, and the program provides a sign-up link for you to share with readers. Readers must create a free AHS account, download your book, and answer any questions you created during the set-up process before they can provide chapter-by-chapter feedback on your book.

Use the ReaderTeam Sign-up Page to manage all aspects of your reader teams.

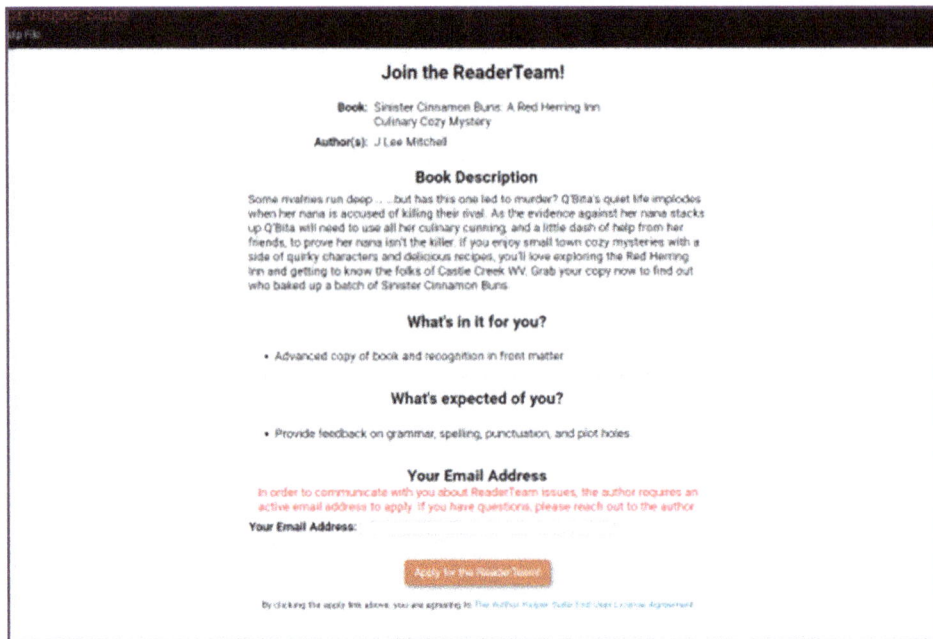

READERLINKS

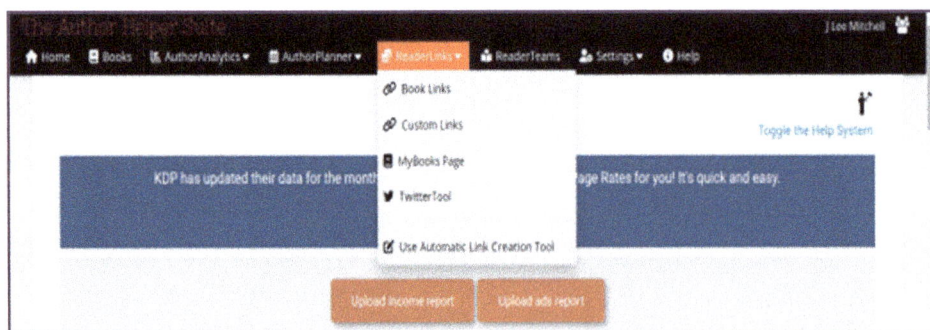

ReaderLinks is the last of the four main features, and many indie authors may already be familiar with it. This tool allows authors to create book-specific links, custom links, and automatic links through AHS's automatic link creation tool.

The ReaderLinks dropdown list contains the Link Creation tools.

BOOK LINKS:

This tool allows authors to create trackable links for individual books or series for each of the sales platforms they utilize. The link allows geolocation or affiliate codes to be added to the end, which is useful for tracking and directing readers to specific country-based platforms, such as Amazon.

CUSTOM LINKS:

As its name implies, this type of link is also customizable, but it doesn't accommodate geolocation or affiliate codes, which makes it better suited as a pointer for non-book-specific locations, such as Facebook or an author's website, where the page remains the same regardless of a reader's location.

AUTOMATIC LINK CREATION TOOL:

This AHS feature saves you time and sanity by automatically creating links that you'll need for every book. Automatic Links let you choose a link design for specific sales channels. The ReaderLinks Robot, RR1, will then use that to automatically set up links for that sales channel for each of your existing books, plus any new books you add later.

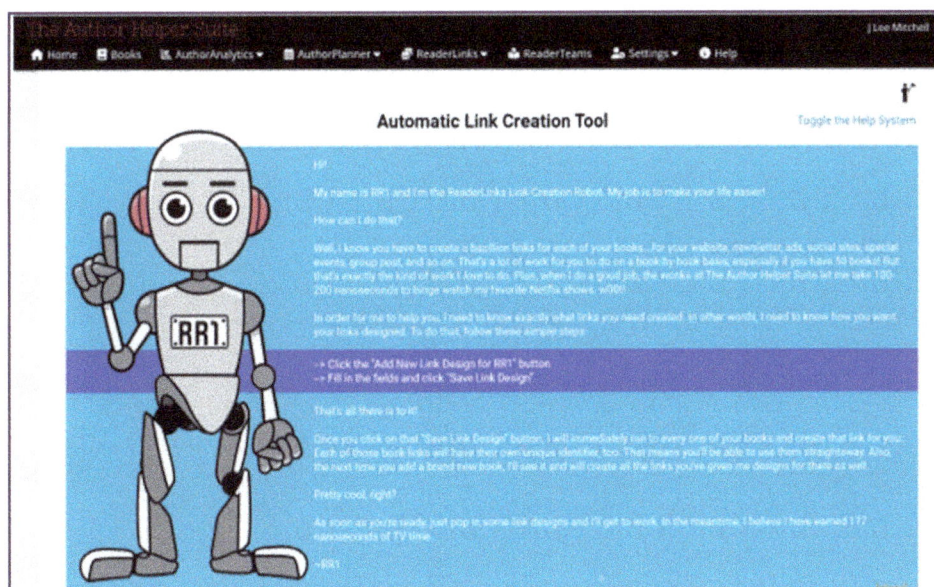

The ReaderLinks RR1 Robot can save you time by automatically creating links for new books and sales channels.

Pro Tip: For authors who use WordPress, the ReaderLinks WordPress plugin allows you to create custom links containing your domain within the link.

This only scratches the surface of everything that AHS has to offer, but one additional feature that really bears mentioning is the ability for authors to set up and track up to three pen names per log-in. This presents a major time-saver for authors and allows you to keep all your data in one place.

WITH SO MANY TOOLS, HOW WILL YOU EVER LEARN TO USE THEM ALL?

As with all new-to-you applications, a learning curve is involved, but AHS shines in this department as well. The phrase "Toggle the Help System" appears in the upper right-hand corner of every page. To view inline help, simply click on the phrase, and instructional tips, directions, and more will appear above each section of the current page. Click the phrase a second time to turn off inline help.

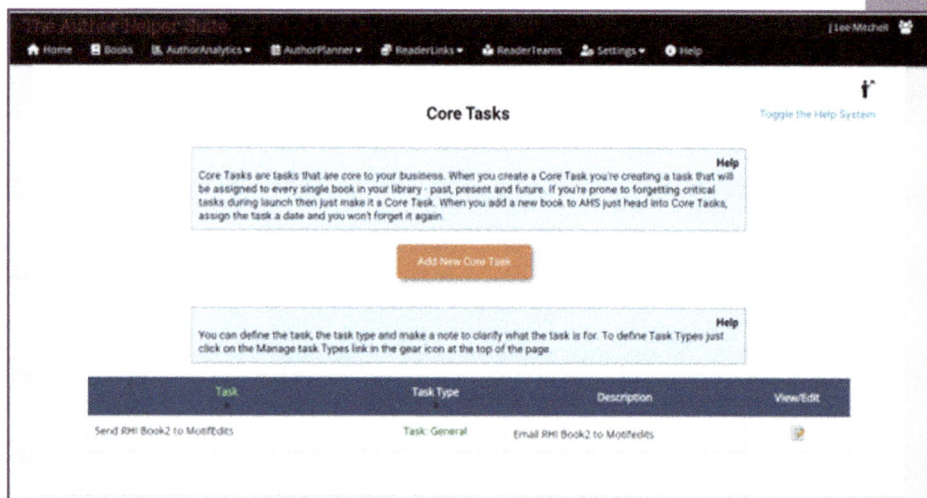

Inline help is available for each page section.

AHS also has a regularly active and engaged Facebook group, The Author Helper Suite | Facebook, with approximately one thousand members where authors can interact, seek assistance, raise issues, and get the lowdown on all things AHS. The group is monitored by its creators, and the response time is fast.

When it comes to learning everything AHS has to offer, the program's newest addition, Author Helper Academy, sets this application apart. Launched June

24, Author Helper Academy is a self-paced, video-based course built on the Teachable platform that walks you through AHS section by section. The brief, high-quality videos feature co-creator John Logsdon and provide a professional quality learning experience that will help you get the most out of AHS.

HOW MUCH DOES IT COST?

AHS was created by indie authors for indie authors, and the platform's developers kept that in mind when designing their pricing structure. According to the site, "We want to be an affordable asset in your business' toolbox. To get the best deal, we ask you to learn about the service and what it can do for you. It's not a traditional pricing structure but we're not a traditional online service!"

As the site suggests, authors can "learn" about the service by taking advantage of the thirty-day free, no-credit-card-required trial. Once the free trial expires, authors have three pricing options to choose from:

- a monthly rate of $24.99
- an annual rate of $239, which costs $60 less per year
- a monthly rate of either $14.99 per month or $179 annually by signing up for AHS's free classes

The AHS Pricing Grid outlines each available package.

With an affordable price point, a robust stable of tools, next-level education, and above-average service, the Author Helper Suite really is the one tool to rule them all. ■

Jenn Mitchell

Tech Tools

Courtesy of IndieAuthorTools.com
Got a tool you love and want to share with us?
Submit a tool at IndieAuthorTools.com

	PUBLISHER ROCKET	https://publisherrocket.com/ Publisher Rocket takes the guesswork out of book promotion on Amazon. Makes no difference whether you're building advertising campaigns, keeping an eye on the competition, or searching for keywords and categories. This tool, formerly known as KDP Rocket, gives you answers in a fraction of the time it'd take you to do the research.
	ADS FOR AUTHORS	https://learn.selfpublishingformula.com/p/adsforauthors Learn how to create profitable ads on some of the largest online platforms – such as Amazon and Facebook – with Mark Dawson's Ads for Authors. This advertising masterclass contains hours of comprehensive video tutorials. An 11-course bundle, this training is suitable for intermediate to advanced level advertisers.
	5-DAY AUTHOR AD PROFIT CHALLENGE	https://www.facebook.com/groups/2230194167089012 Each quarter, Bryan Cohen and his team run the free 5-Day Author Ad Profit Challenge. In addition to live support, the event provides hours of video walk-throughs and instruction to teach authors how to run more profitable Amazon Ads. "Advertising can be scary," Cohen says. "But when you focus on only the essential numbers like royalties and ad spend, it becomes a whole lot simpler."
	BOOK BRUSH	https://bookbrush.com/ Simplify the creation of social media images and high-quality professional ads with Book Brush. This user-friendly, time-saving design tool has numerous features created specifically for authors. Even the non-artistic ones. You can try it out for free, but to create more than 15 images and upload fonts, you'll need the Plus plan.
	AMAZON ALGO-RITHMS	https://blog.reedsy.com/learning/courses/marketing/amazon-algorithms/ In this Reedsy Learning course, Ricardo Fayet will help you "understand how the Amazon recommendation machine works and give you the knowledge to make it work to your advantage." The free 10-part training is delivered daily to your inbox.

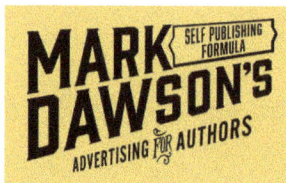

Join the Club

WHAT WRITERS CAN GAIN FROM CLUBHOUSE, THE AUDIO-ONLY SOCIAL NETWORK

2020 was a pivotal year for everyone. COVID quarantines had people scrambling for things to do, especially creatives. For writers, book signings were postponed indefinitely. Screenwriters watched as filming around the globe halted, and life generally took a dystopian turn. More than ever, networking on social media took center stage as we strived to keep up our relationships and develop new ones.

Insert Clubhouse, the audio-only social media app. From the beginning, Clubhouse distinguished itself as a new way to network with people around the world. At first, it operated more like a secret society, with only iPhone users having access and membership requiring an ever-elusive invitation. According to its website, Clubhouse operated as an "invite only" club to accommodate its growth during the beta-testing phase. Soon enough, the app opened up to Android users and, more recently, new members no longer needed an invitation to join.

Still, many writers are unfamiliar with the app or unsure how to use it for networking. As a less common platform, Clubhouse can easily fall into the trap of being viewed as just one more app for authors to contend with among other marketing tools like Facebook, Twitter, and TikTok. But Clubhouse truly fills in a unique space and can help your author career should you choose to use it.

Once you've downloaded the app, you'll input your bio, photo, and interests. Despite being audio only, first impressions make all the difference. An eye-catching bio is key. Including links to your books, website, and other social media accounts is a must, but you'll also want to give new acquaintances a reason to visit them. Some authors include a couple of book titles or short Bitly links to their latest releases, but don't keep it all business. Write out some fun facts you want others to know about you. If you have a longer bio or more information you want to impart, do it in bullet-point form using a fun emoji for each new item.

After you've set up your profile, the next step is finding others with whom you can network. The best way to do this is to use the search feature at the top of the page and search for clubs that meet your interests. For instance, the Writing Room connects writers through workshops and other rooms, and Writing For Your Life includes rooms with industry guests to provide advice and tips on just about anything writing related. If you want to focus on sprint writing, the club Write That Thang provides all the sprints you can ask for. You can also find clubs based on your particular genre that talk about everything regarding your interests.

After you've found some clubs to join, start exploring rooms, the meeting places within each club. These rooms are live, but you can also find recorded sessions if the moderators allow it for that room. You can find recordings on the club's main page within the app. There, you can also find information on upcoming scheduled rooms, although a member of a club can host a pop-up room at any time.

Upon entering a room, you are automatically placed in the audience section. Above the audience section is the stage, where speakers reside. The ones with a green asterisk are moderators, and others on stage are people who have come up from the audience to ask questions or talk. Some rooms are more informal, where everyone is on stage chit-chatting, but most rooms operate in the stage/audience format. If you have something to say or ask, you'll raise your hand, or unmute yourself, at the bottom right corner of the screen. A moderator will pull you up, and you will automatically be on mute. To speak during your turn, you will need to unmute yourself, then re-mute once you're done speaking.

One of the biggest mistakes a person makes when on stage in a room is to give their bio and ask others in the room—especially moderators—if they'll review something they've written or tell them they are looking for a particular type of writing gig. Just as you wouldn't walk up to someone randomly and do this, you wouldn't want to brag about yourself or beg for work when networking. Instead, stick to the topic. If you're first asked to introduce yourself and say what you do, keep it brief. If listeners want to know more, they will look at your bio and possibly follow you. Also, when in a room, even if you're not speaking, it's courtesy to follow all moderators. If an audience member on stage talks about something you're interested in, check out their bio and follow them. They will probably follow you back, and you will have begun an integral part of networking: following others and gaining new followers.

After attending enough rooms, others will get to know you and invite you to join additional smaller clubs where you can get to chat with more writers and industry leaders. The more rooms you participate in, the more opportunities you will have to meet others. You also do not just have to attend rooms on writing. Finding other writing rooms or rooms in the areas of your interests, such as movie watch parties or book discussions, can help you meet new acquaintances and friends. You're also not limited to joining rooms. Start your own rooms, especially those with a specific topic to discuss or debate, and others will join in. You can do this on your own or find others to co-host a room with you.

Just as with the larger rooms, if you're in a smaller room with acquaintances, don't brag about your work or solicit connections. An additional must: Don't lie about yourself. Amazon, IMDb, and Google are powerful tools, and it's all too easy to check someone out. If you're giving false information or inflating your résumé, that person will automatically

blacklist you. And because people on Clubhouse talk, if you enter a room with someone you've misrepresented your career to, they will let others know.

Although others will vet you via the Internet, you'll also want to do the same to them. If someone approaches you about working together, do your homework first to verify they are who they say they are. And like with any other social media or networking, before you send anything for someone to review after they've requested, send that all-important NDA first. Also, just as you wouldn't send a publisher or agent an unsolicited manuscript, do not send an unsolicited manuscript or screenplay to another writer, publisher, director, or industry expert. Wait until you receive an invitation.

Although the list of dos and don'ts is large, many have found success networking through Clubhouse. "Like anything with the entertainment industry, you have to weed out a lot of talkers and people claiming to things they are not, but Clubhouse has been a great resource to connect with writers from all over the world," says Gavin Michael Booth, writer, producer, and director of *The Scarehouse* and *Last Call*. "I've found two co-writers for feature scripts as well as been attached to direct two other short films from writers I first met on Clubhouse."

Networking on Clubhouse can be daunting at first, but it is an important part of social media with which writers are largely unfamiliar. When following the unspoken regulations of the app, one can not only make new writer and reader friends but also find huge opportunities for their career—all the more reason to join and start exploring a whole new corner of the world.

Angie Martin

Get documents done anywhere

Now available for your Android & iOS mobile device

Dragon® Anywhere professional-grade mobile dictation makes it easy to create documents of any length, edit, format and share them directly from your mobile device-whether visiting clients, a job site, or your local coffee shop.

- Continuous dictation and no word limits
- 99% accurate with powerful voice editing and formatting
- Access customized words and auto-text across all devices
- Share documents by email, Dropbox, Evernote and more

Select a flexible pricing plan Subscribe now ▾

*Credit Card Required. After your 7 day free trial, the monthly subscription begins at $15 per month. Cancel at anytime.

WriteLink.To/Dragon

Podcasts We Love

PIN TO TOP

https://podcasts.apple.com/us/podcast/pin-to-top/id1454163881

Looking for Facebook marketing basics, strategies, or tactics? Check out the weekly Pin To Top, hosted by social media marketing strategist Ann Kristine Peñaredondo. "Growing your business doesn't have to be overwhelming," she says. "I can help you be on top of the changing Facebook algorithms, trends, and updates."

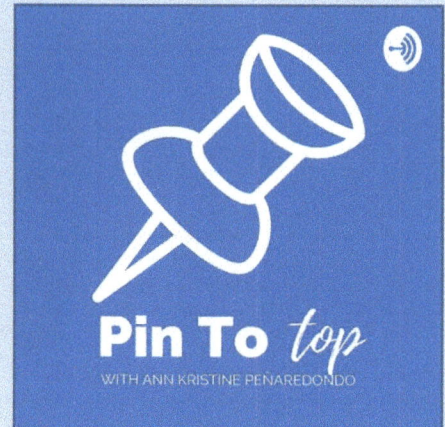

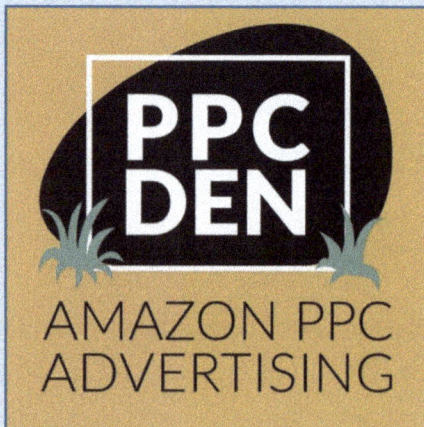

PPC DEN: AMAZON PPC ADVERTISING MASTERY

https://podcasts.apple.com/us/podcast/ppc-den-amazon-ppc-advertising-mastery/id1439688182

The world's first Amazon advertising podcast – hosted by Ad Badger. Here we discuss the ins and outs of Amazon PPC, including tips and tricks to help optimize your ad campaigns. Whether you're a die-hard [pay-per-click] fanatic or an Amazon seller looking for an edge, this is the podcast for you.

NEXT LEVEL FACEBOOK ADS PODCAST

http://fbadspodcast.com/

This show appeals to veteran Facebook advertisers as well as beginners with its mix of content. The weekly show, hosted by Phil Graham, drops on Tuesdays with the latest tips "to help you stand out from the noise and leverage Facebook Ads for your success."

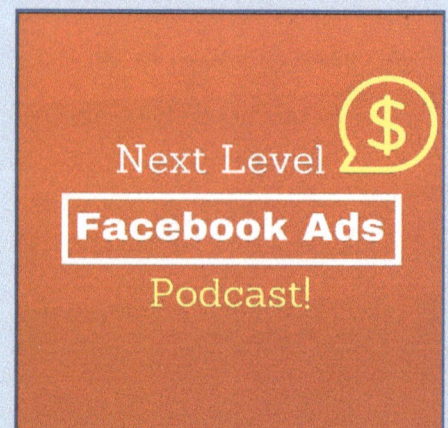

From the Mouths of Babes

THE ART OF WRITING HOW CHILDREN SPEAK

Let's face it: Kids are a lot of work. No one would argue that point in the real world—no one who's spent time around them, anyhow. And little ones can be just as much of a handful on the page. Especially when it comes to dialogue, making young characters believable can leave a thin margin for error. According to Novelists, Inc. (https://ninc.com), writers often lean either too eloquent or too "cutesy" to make them sound authentic. In a guest post for the Jane Friedman writing blog (https://janefriedman. com), developmental editor Jessi Hoffman even ventures to say kids' speech is some of the worst dialogue ever written.

For authors who interact with children regularly through their day jobs or via family and friends, writing dialogue is somewhat easier—as long as characters and their real-life counterparts are around the same age. But there's a more consistent way to craft dialogue for children. Both the National Institute on Deafness and Other Communication Disorders (NIDCD) and the American Speech-Language-Hearing Association (ASHA) list benchmarks for children's speech development based on their age. No need for extra babysitting gigs—just match your character's dialogue to the proper language milestones.

BIRTH

In the first few months of their life, babies don't do much in the way of intelligent speech. At this stage, both ASHA and NIDCD list cooing, crying, giggling, and babbling as typical. Around six months old, children might also begin to use gestures, such as raising their arms to be lifted or waving bye, and they'll start to understand the word "no" and their name, according to ASHA. Within their first year, according to NIDCD, they might also say their first word, though this would generally happen closer to their first birthday.

ONE YEAR OLD

At one year old, children will begin to point to body parts when asked and may begin to ask simple questions themselves, such as "what?" or "where?" According to NIDCD, their vocabulary should grow to about fifty words, though they might not always be easily understood.

1

TWO YEARS OLD

Children have a word for almost everything by two years old and will start to understand opposites, ASHA lists, and they will have developed object permanence. They'll also begin to ask the dreaded "why?"

Their speech may still leave off some ending sounds, according to NIDCD, but they can generally be understood by their family or those close to them.

2

THREE YEARS OLD

Toddlers begin to match rhyming words and separate things into groups around three years old, according to ASHA. They'll use pronouns like "I," "me," "you," or "they" and start to express ideas and feelings rather than just make visual observations. According to NIDCD, at this stage, children will start to have fun with language and recognize silly statements in books or jokes.

3

FOUR YEARS OLD

4

At four years old and beyond, children will begin to tell stories and answer complex questions. Their speech is understandable, according to NIDCD, though they might still make some mistakes when pronouncing long words—think about how Nemo struggles with "anemone" in *Finding Nemo*.

They'll use some irregular past tense verbs at this stage, so try to avoid the misplaced "-ed" endings on words like "fall" or "sit." They'll also speak differently with different people, using shorter and simpler sentences with younger children while asking adults more complicated, inquisitive questions, according to ASHA.

A FINAL NOTE: SPEECH DISORDERS AND OTHER DISABILITIES

Not every child develops exactly along this timeline, so not every character needs to either. A toddler in your story with a disability, a stutter, or other speech disorder could regress in some milestones, meet them at a slower pace, or miss them entirely. It's impossible to list specific symptoms for every diagnosis here, but according to Maryville University, common signs of speech disorders include sound substitutions, additions, or omissions; speaking in a strange pitch; or using gestures to communicate instead of words.

Dialogue is never one-size-fits-all, even for younger characters, and sometimes a wise-beyond-their-years observation or an embarrassing question will be more believable than a mispronounced word. As with anything, do your research, and if it comes to it, don't be afraid to draw from real-life experiences. After all, it's not just a saying—kids truly do say the darndest things. ■

Nicole Schroeder

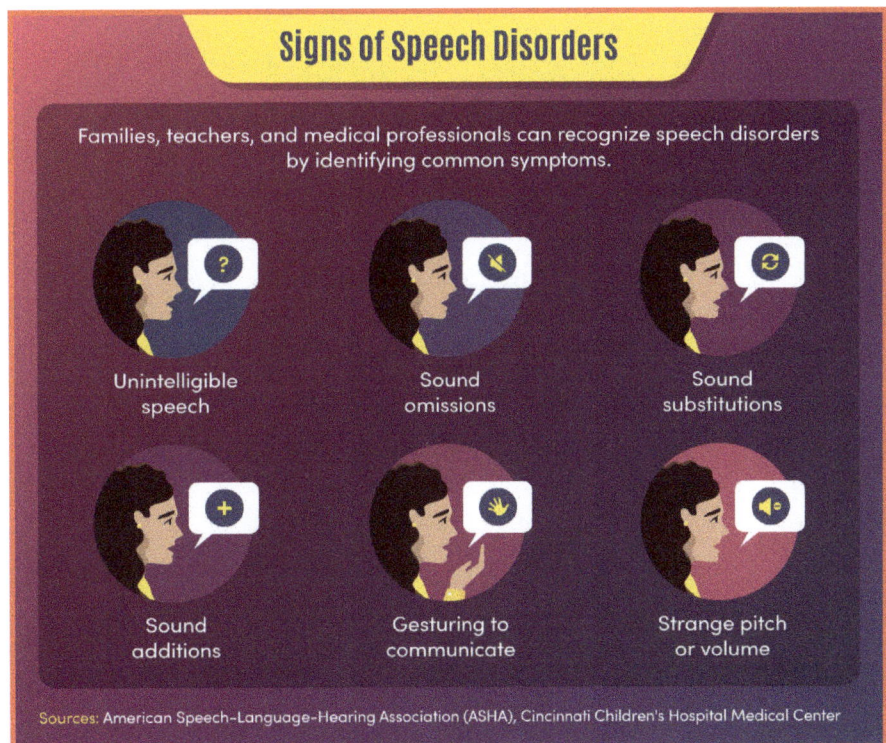

Signs of Speech Disorders

Families, teachers, and medical professionals can recognize speech disorders by identifying common symptoms.

Unintelligible speech

Sound omissions

Sound substitutions

Sound additions

Gesturing to communicate

Strange pitch or volume

Sources: American Speech-Language-Hearing Association (ASHA), Cincinnati Children's Hospital Medical Center

Know the Lingo

NEW ADULT VERSUS YOUNG ADULT FICTION

We all know what a "young adult" is—after all, we've all been one. But as it turns out, we've all been "new adults" as well, a lesser-known age range that directly follows young adulthood. Over the years, both "young adult" and "new adult" stages of life have sparked genres of the same names, and though the two terms sound similar, whether discussing the age ranges or the fiction representing them, the two couldn't be more unique.

New Adult (NA) is a developing area in the publishing industry. The term was first used by St. Martin's Press in 2009, when the publisher put out a call looking for submissions for "fiction similar to YA that can be published and marketed as adult—a sort of an 'older YA' or 'new adult' … with protagonists who are slightly older than YA and can appeal to an adult audience," according to an archived version of the publisher's website.

NA is an age category that comes directly after Young Adult (YA). However, because NA is still in its nascent stages, authors and readers alike often confuse the two. NA—like its counterparts, YA, Middle Grade, and Adult—encompasses many genres and subgenres. Although an author could write both YA Contemporary Romance and NA Contemporary Romance, the two are vastly different.

So what are the similarities and differences between NA and YA?

PROTAGONIST'S AGE

In YA, protagonists tend to be on the younger side. They are typically aged between fifteen and eighteen years old. NA, on the other hand, skews slightly older: Protagonists usually range from eighteen to twenty-five and, in some cases, up to thirty years old.

SETTING

Stories with teenage characters are usually, though not always, set in or feature a high school or academy. Even if the protagonist has left school early, there is typically a reason for this. NA stories tend to be set in college or graduate school after the character has left home. NA stories can also feature characters getting and settling into their first jobs or internships.

However, academy settings could feature in both YA and NA. In these stories, the char-

acter's age, the type of academy—a high school or secondary school academy versus a college-type academy—and themes are usually solid indicators of whether the story is classified as YA or NA.

HEAT LEVEL

YA tends to skew toward Sweet or Clean Romance. First love and teenage angst are often seen in YA, and the heat level follows accordingly. At most, YA features fade-to-black scenes with a focus on the emotional impact on the characters rather than the physical.

NA, on the other hand, tends to have more room for spice. Open-door scenes with a focus on both the physical and the emotional are not uncommon. That said, just because a story is classified as NA does not automatically imply heat or spice.

THEMES

The difference in age between YA and NA protagonists tends to correspond to the differing themes present in both age categories.

YA stories are often about coming of age and

focus on themes such as finding one's place in the world or first relationships, along with a healthy dose of teen angst. NA fiction, on the other hand, tends to focus on characters leaving home for the first time, their education or career choices, first jobs and internships, and finding their sexuality, engagement, or marriage. In NA, the protagonist takes the first steps outside the comfort of their home, learning to navigate the troubled waters of adulthood.

MARKETING

As NA is a developing age category, the difference between YA and NA fiction is not always obvious, especially on retailers like Amazon.

Crucially, the NA category does not exist on major book retailers, including Amazon, which, like most distributors, uses the Book Industry Standards and Communications (BISAC) classification system, one of the world's most common book classification systems. NA does not feature on the BISAC Subject Headings list. And no feature on BISAC means there's no category with distributors.

As a result, NA authors tend to categorize their NA books as YA. It's not just the indies—it's the big publishers as well. A well-known publisher placed a famous NA fantasy series in the YA category, and those books were even

chosen as "Editor's Picks" for YA.

Due to the differences between YA and NA outlined above, the lack of NA on the BISAC Subject Headings list is creating widespread problems, and the ripple effects are felt by both YA and NA authors and readers. If a reader browsing the YA categories on their favorite retailer is searching for a clean story about a teen saving the world and instead gets a story with heavy romance and spice because the book is classified as YA on the distributor's site, they won't be happy. This could, in turn, lead to negative reviews, thereby hurting everyone in the process.

So what can authors do?

First, ask BISAC to add NA to its list of Subject Headings and allow the change to trickle down to Amazon and other major retailers. The BISAC website has a helpful suggestion form. In the meantime, to avoid further confusion, NA authors should look into delisting their NA books from YA categories or prevent confusion from happening in the first place by placing their books in the adult categories—that is, until such a time when NA becomes an officially recognized subject heading by BISAC. ■

Kasia Lasinska

Different Strokes

DIFFERENT STROKES" AND THE SUBHEAD TO "MIX UP YOUR WRITING METHODS WITH THESE TYPING ALTERNATIVES

We love being authors, but sometimes we can't or don't want to be click-clacking on keys for hours day after day. It could be for health and mobility issues or the desire to be more productive during your commute or while waiting at the doctor's office. If you're like me, it could be that you were never much of a typist and wrote your first books longhand in a five-subject notebook—or moleskins and sketchbooks, like those I use now. But I digress.

If you want to mix up your writing methods, here are two great options.

SPEECH TO TEXT

Much like dictation software, speech to text gives you a hands-free way to get your words on the page. Unlike dictation, where you're talking into a microphone in real time, with speech to text, you can record your words for the day on your phone, drop the MP3 into the web app, and let it transcribe.

This is perfect when you're doing another activity, such as driving or taking a walk, and want to get your words in as long as you're not worried people will hear you talking through your story.

Consider the length of your MP3 and whether you need language support or translation.

Pro Tip: Speechnotes is great with long recordings, and it's free.

WRITING ON A TABLET

Apple Scribble lets those who handwrite like me use the Apple pencil to jot down ideas in any app that accepts text on the iPad. It works well with Apple Pages and Google Docs. You will have to learn some gestures for functions like cut and paste, new lines, changing fonts, and the like, but with a little practice, these become second nature.

Another option is reMarkable, a thin profile tablet that's designed for writing longhand and can sync with cloud storage like Google Drive, Dropbox, or Microsoft OneDrive for a monthly fee.

Typing alternatives can increase your output and production levels so that you are that much closer to the ultimate goal: releasing your next book. ■

Chrishaun Keller-Hanna

The Silent Struggle

A LOOK AT THE RELATIONSHIP BETWEEN WRITING AND MENTAL HEALTH

As always, if you suffer from mental illness, these tips are not a substitute for seeking proper professional treatment. If you are in immediate danger with suicidal thoughts or tendencies, please do one of the following: Contact the National Suicide Hotline at 988-273-8255, call a local hotline, contact 911 to have an ambulance sent to your location, or seek immediate treatment at the closest emergency room. You can contact NAMI at 800-950-NAMI (6264) or live chat with them on their website, https://nami.org.

According to the National Alliance on Mental Illness (NAMI), one in five adults in the US have experienced mental illness at some point in their life. Writers and other creative types, however, suffer at much greater rates than the average American. Over a decade of studies show the following approximate statistics for authors and artists:

- Between 5 and 40 percent experience bipolar disorder.
- Between 15 and 50 percent have major depressive disorder.
- They carry twice the risk for schizophrenia.
- They are twice as likely to commit suicide.

These statistics are based only on what is reported, so true numbers could be higher. And though many strides have been made to erase the stigma of mental illness, a diagnosis can still carry shame for many sufferers. This can affect the average person in their daily life, but it can hinder a writer's ability to write and affect their career. What can authors do to not only survive mental illness but to also channel their ailments to assist their writing?

Good news! Some believe having a mental illness can actually contribute to great writing. According to Psychology Today (https://psychologytoday.com), "Mental health professionals have observed the therapeutic effects of writing on patients with schizophrenia—finding that the creative process assists these individuals with managing their symptoms."

Writing has long been considered a cathartic process. Edgar Allen Poe is known for having multiple mental illnesses at a time when psychology didn't widely recognize them or have proper treatment in place. He is known for saying in a fan letter, "I became insane, with long intervals of horrible sanity." And he isn't the only famous author to suffer.

Knowing one is not alone is always the first line of defense against mental illness. More authors and creatives are also speaking openly about their battles. Not everyone is equipped to discuss their afflictions publicly, but if you are one of them, you can help countless others who suffer in addition to providing an outlet to cleanse your mind.

This is the first in a series of three articles discussing mental illness and the role it can play in an author's career. ■

Angie Martin

Set Yourself Up for Anthology Success

Nearly all writers want to make new author friends and boost their book marketing. One great way to do this is by writing for an anthology. But you should be aware of possible pitfalls before you take part, and it's best to have a plan.

DEFINING AN ANTHOLOGY

An anthology is a book containing a collection of short stories or a mix of poetry, prose, and other writing. You may also hear people refer to a box set, which is more often a collection of complete novellas or full-length books.

Story word counts vary for anthologies and box sets, going from a hundred words for a drabble right up to 70,000 words or more for a full-length story.

Most anthologies focus on a particular genre, such as YA, Urban Fantasy, or Steamy Romance. There's usually a theme and/or a trope, such as summer nights or enemies to lovers. Authors might also find shared world opportunities where everyone gets to write a story set in the same world.

In addition, anthologies have different aims, including charity sets to raise money for a particular cause, money-making sets, sets to get your new pen name out there, sets to go wide, and list-aiming sets.

AN OVERVIEW OF THE PROCESS

Some anthologies are free to join, and some have a buy-in amount. If there is a buy-in fee, the set coordinator may take a percentage of the sales too—usually between 10 percent and 20 percent. Buy-ins can range from around ten dollars to over five hundred dollars for list-aim sets. List-aim sets often come with an expectation that you'll also provide a marketing budget for ads and promotional sites.

A contract will also lay out important dates and other information, such as royalty shares, whether the anthology will be published wide or through Kindle Unlimited, payment dates, when your rights will be returned to you, the final deadline for submissions, and the release date.

If you sign up for a set with an experienced coordinator, then you'll find a quality cover is included, and everything is organized for you. Some marketing might also already be in place, perhaps from paid ads or promotional sites.

Some organizers set up a group for the anthology so you have one place to go for updates, questions, polls, and all the information you need. The coordinator may have a way to organize and assign different jobs involved in running and marketing an anthology. Along with everyone else, you will be expected to promote the anthology, including on your social media and in your newsletter. The organizer may also allocate jobs, such as running BookFunnel promotions, arranging BookBub review and buy swaps, and posting in appropriate genre Facebook groups.

If you've never done this before and don't know what some of those tasks are or how to do them, don't be shy about asking your coordinator. They'd rather explain and help you than have you not market the anthology as part of the group.

Some organizers let people post on their own schedule while others have a schedule for posts and newsletters. You may find that your organizer offers extra marketing for a fee, so you don't have to post as much. Still, be aware that it does take time to post and keep up with the related duties. You'll need to organize these around your writing and everything else you have to do daily.

The amount of work involved varies depending on the type of anthology. As you might imagine, a list-aiming anthology will involve several hours every week with potentially more time requirements as release week nears.

As long as you keep up to date and stay involved in your group or chat, you shouldn't have a problem knowing what to do next. And if you do, your organizer is there to help.

WHAT TO LOOK OUT FOR

You need to do your homework on your anthology organizer and make sure they know what they're doing. There are horror stories of organizers taking the buy-in money and disappearing or never paying out royalties.

Know who will be receiving your buy-in before you sign up. Check in with other authors and anthology organizers to make sure your chosen coordinator is trustworthy.

Check your contract and run it past a lawyer. Make sure there's nothing problematic in there, such as rights grabs, where the organizer is trying to claim your audio rights, movie rights, or more. An April 2015 article by Helen Sedwick of The Book Designer includes detailed information on how to spot rights grabs in your contracts: https://tinyurl.com/BookDesigner.

HOW TO CHOOSE YOUR ANTHOLOGIES

Ask yourself whether a particular anthology fits your author plan. Will it advance your author goals? There are so many anthologies to choose from that it's like being a kid in a candy store. But you can't write for all of them, nor should you.

When picking an anthology, it's a great idea to make sure it either fits with what you already write or would be an opportunity to introduce a new pen name in a new genre. Perhaps you could use the anthology to write a lead magnet for your newsletter, a prequel to an existing series, or an introduction to the next series you'd like to write. It's much easier to market related stories and gain read-through to your other books. However, it is up to you. If you enjoy writing stories in multiple genres, then why not have fun with it as long as you have room in your schedule? Doing so can be a fun way to try out new genres.

MAKE THE MOST OF YOUR PARTICIPATION

You can take a few more steps to ensure you get everything you can out of involvement in anthologies, box sets, and shared worlds.

- **Whitelist the organizer's emails.** That will ensure you're getting all the information you need. Join the anthology group, chat, or social media page, and get to know everyone. Don't be afraid to ask questions of project organizers or offer to help if you can.
- **Stay organized.** When you're part of many anthologies, it's easy to miss a deadline or a takeover party. Note everything on your calendar.

- **Do your part.** Some people join anthologies and don't do a stroke of marketing. They don't post, join the group, or help anyone. Don't be that person. Not only will you not get the most out of it, but anthology coordinators do talk and share. Do this regularly, and you'll wear out your welcome.
- **Stick to the deadlines.** Coordinators shouldn't need to chase you for your story at the last minute. Sometimes things come up, and you can't get your story in on time, but try not to make a habit of being late or of dropping out of sets. Again, organizers talk.
- **Set up your back matter.** With most anthologies, you will have space for a short bio and some links. Use this to your advantage: Include both your newsletter sign-up link so people can get on your mailing list and your Amazon page link so readers can see what else you have to offer. Include a blurb and buying link to any books and preorders that are related to your anthology story. Just be sure to stick to the format and number of links allotted by the anthology organizer.

With a plan in place and careful selection of your anthologies, you can enjoy new author connections and advance your author career in fresh ways.

WHERE TO FIND ANTHOLOGIES

To find anthologies you can join, talk to authors you know about anthologies they've been in. Facebook groups aplenty offer anthology, box set, and shared world opportunities.

Here are just some of them:

- Boxed Set Opportunities for Authors: https://facebook.com/groups/BoxedSetOpps
- Margo's Group for Authors—Boxed Sets: https://facebook.com/groups/boxedsetsforauthors
- Anthologies and Collections for Indie Authors: https://facebook.com/groups/anthologiesandcollections
- Amaryllis Media Open Calls & Marketing Opportunities: https://.facebook.com/groups/amaryllismedia ◼

Gill Fernley

From the Stacks

Courtesy of IndieAuthorTools.com
Got a book you love and want to share with us?
Submit a book at IndieAuthorTools.com

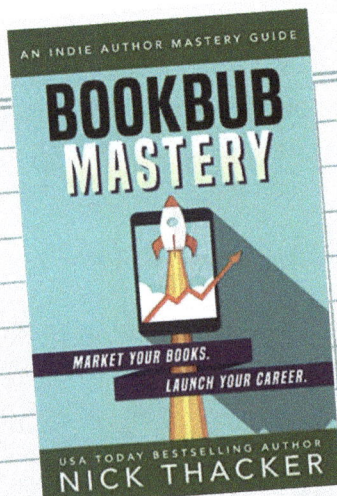

BookBub Mastery: An Indie Author Mastery Guide

https://books2read.com/u/bp8Lyg

In this concise guide, Nick Thacker shares the strategy he has developed for obtaining BookBub Featured Deals. "Featured Deals are hard to come by, and some authors swear they're impossible to get," Thacker says. "I'm here to tell those authors that it is possible, and it's probably likely … If you have a plan."

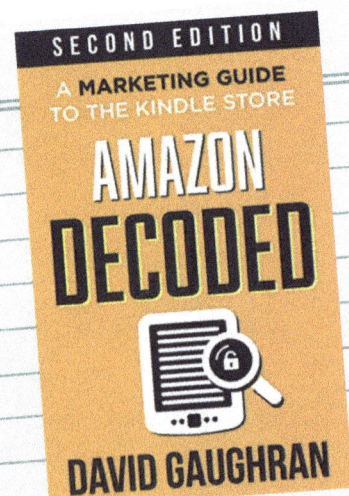

Amazon Decoded: A Marketing Guide to the Kindle Store (Second Edition)

https://books2read.com/u/bw1pyG

Want to better understand the dynamics that will help you sell more books in the Kindle store? Or even better, have Amazon do much of the selling for you? *Amazon Decoded: A Marketing Guide to the Kindle Store* by David Gaughran will show you how.

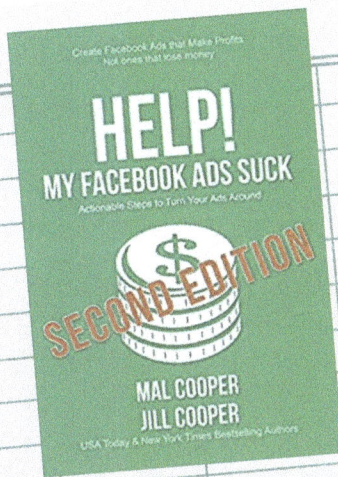

Help! My Facebook Ads Suck: Second Edition
https://books2read.com/u/3G5jVQ

Confused by Facebook advertising? Break through the overwhelm with *Help! My Facebook Ads Suck: Second Edition*. This concise, easy-to-read book takes you step-by-step through the process. Although last updated in December, 2019, the advertising guide is still an excellent source of golden nuggets. The authors also have a free Facebook group – The Writing Wives Ads & Marketing Group.

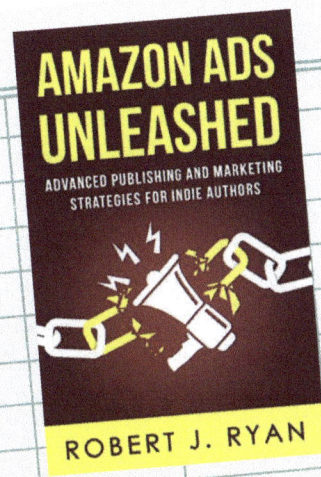

Amazon Ads for Indie Authors: A How-to Guide from an Industry Expert
https://books2read.com/u/4X690v

Former Amazon Advertising manager Janet Margot shares how to create, manage and optimize book ads in *Amazon Ads for Indie Authors*. This concise guide will help you simplify your approach to the retail giant. Whether you want to learn how to create a basic ad or to avoid costly mistakes, you'll find valuable information.

Amazon Ads Unleashed: Advanced Publishing and Marketing Strategies for Indie Authors
https://books2read.com/u/3y1GWn

Amazon Ads Unleashed goes beyond algorithms to highlight buyer behavior. "This is an advanced guide to mastering Amazon ads by a six-figure-author who makes his living from writing and advertising his books," says Robert J. Ryan, who updated this book in 2021.

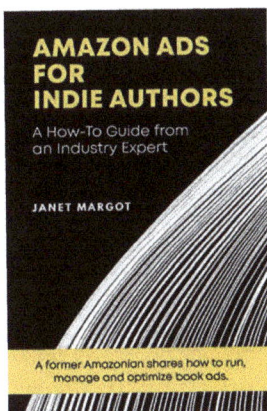

In This Issue

Executive Team

Chelle Honiker, Publisher

As the publisher of Indie Author Magazine, Chelle Honiker brings nearly three decades of startup, technology, training, and executive leadership experience to the role. She's a serial entrepreneur, founding and selling multiple successful companies including a training development company, travel agency, website design and hosting firm, a digital marketing consultancy, and a wedding planning firm. She's organized and curated multiple TEDx events and hired to assist other nonprofit organizations as a fractional executive, including The Travel Institute and The Freelance Association.

As a writer, speaker, and trainer she believes in the power of words and their ability to heal, inspire, incite, and motivate. Her greatest inspiration is her daughters, Kelsea and Cathryn, who tolerate her tendency to run away from home to play with her friends around the world for months at a time. It's said she could run a small country with just the contents of her backpack.

Alice Briggs, Creative Director

As the creative director of Indie Author Magazine, Alice Briggs utilizes her more than three decades of artistic exploration and expression, business startup adventures, and leadership skills. A serial entrepreneur, she has started several successful businesses. She brings her experience in creative direction, magazine layout and design, and graphic design in and outside of the indie author community to her role.

With a masters of science in Occupational Therapy, she has a broad skill set and uses it to assist others in achieving their desired goals. As a writer, teacher, healer, and artist, she loves to see people accomplish all they desire. She's excited to see how IAM will encourage many authors to succeed in whatever way they choose. She hopes to meet many of you in various places around the world once her passport is back in use.

Nicole Schroeder, Editor in Chief

Nicole Schroeder is a storyteller at heart. As the editor in chief of Indie Author Magazine, she brings nearly a decade of journalism and editorial experience to the publication, delighting in any opportunity to tell true stories and help others do the same. She holds a bachelor's degree from the Missouri School of Journalism and minors in English and Spanish. Her previous work includes editorial roles at local publications, and she's helped edit and produce numerous fiction and nonfiction books, including a Holocaust survivor's memoir, alongside independent publishers. Her own creative writing has been published in national literary magazines. When she's not at her writing desk, Nicole is usually in the saddle, cuddling her guinea pigs, or spending time with family. She loves any excuse to talk about Marvel movies and considers National Novel Writing Month its own holiday.

Writers

Angela Archer

Having worked as a mental health nurse for many years, Angela combines her love of words with her love of human psychology to work as a copywriter in the UK. She independently published a novella and novel in 2020 and is currently fending off the lure of shiny new novel ideas to complete the second book in her sci-fi series.

When she's not tinkering with words, she's usually drinking tea, playing the saxophone (badly), or being mum and wife to her husband and two boys.

Bradley Charbonneau

Bradley Charbonneau wanted to be a writer. Trouble was, he didn't write. A friend was running a "Monthly Experiment" (no coffee for a month, wake up at 5 AM, etc.) and created one where everyone had to write every single day for 30 days. Bradley took the challenge. "Hmm, that wasn't so bad." Then he kept going. 100 days. 365. 1,000. 2,808 days and 31 books later and he found out it's simple. Not necessarily easy, but simple. #write #everysingleday

Gill Fernley

Gill Fernley writes fiction in several genres under different pen names, but what all of them have in common is humour and romance, because she can't resist a happy ending or a good laugh. She's also a freelance content writer and has been running her own business since 2013. Before that, she was a technical author and documentation manager for an engineering company and can describe to you more than you'd ever wish to know about airflow and filtration in downflow booths. Still awake? Wow, that's a first! Anyway, that experience taught her how to explain complex things in straightforward language and she hopes it will come in handy for writing articles for IAM. Outside of writing, she's a cake decorator, expert shoe hoarder, and is fluent in English, dry humour and procrastibaking.

Natalie Hobbs

My name is Natalie Hobbs and I am a Journalism major from Houston, TX. I am a senior at Texas Tech University and will be graduating this August. My favorite things to do are spend time with my two dogs and family, cook, and go shopping! After college, I want to work in the influencer marketing field and eventually open up my own non-profit.

Chrishaun Keller-Hanna

Chrishaun Keller-Hanna is an award-winning journalist, teacher, technical writer, and fiction author that lives for explaining difficult concepts in a way that non-technical readers can understand. She spent twenty years teaching literacy and composition to a variety of students from kindergarten to college level and writing technical documentation for several tech companies in the Austin area. At the age of forty-three, she decided to write fiction and has published over thirty titles so far with plans to extend out to comics and board games.

When she's not writing, she's traveling, playing video games, or watching movies. When she's not doing THAT, she's talking about them with her husband and grown daughters.

Kasia Lasinska

Kasia Lasinska holds an LLB in Law with European Legal Studies and an LL.M. in Advanced Studies in International Law. As a practicing attorney, Kasia worked with a top international human rights barrister and then advised clients at a large, international law firm. These inspired her to write dystopian and fantasy novels about corrupt governments and teenagers saving the world.

Kasia has lived in eight countries and speaks five languages (fluently after a glass of wine). She currently lives in London, but her daydreams are filled with beaches and palm trees.

When she's not writing, you can find Kasia scouting out the best coffee shops in town, planning her next great adventure, or petting other people's puppies.

Megan Linski-Fox

Megan Linski lives in Michigan. She is a USA TODAY Bestselling Author and the author of more than fifty novels. She has over fifteen years of experience writing books alongside working as a journalist and editor. She graduated from the University of Iowa, where she studied Creative Writing.

Megan advocates for the rights of the disabled, and is an activist for mental health awareness. She co-writes the Hidden Legends Universe with Alicia Rades. She also writes under the pen name of Natalie Erin for the Creatures of the Lands series, co-authored by Krisen Lison.

Angie Martin

Award-winning author Angie Martin has spent over a decade mentoring and helping new and experienced authors as they prepare to send their babies into the world. She relies on her criminal justice background and knack for researching the tiniest of details to assist others when crafting their own novels. She has given countless speeches in various aspects of writing, including creating characters, self-publishing, and writing supernatural and paranormal. She also assisted in leading a popular California writers' group, which organized several book signings for local authors. In addition to having experience in film, she created the first interactive murder mystery on Clubhouse and writes and directs each episode. Angie now resides in rural Tennessee, where she continues to help authors around the world in every stage of publication while writing her own thriller and horror books, as well as branching out into new genres.

Craig Martelle

High school Valedictorian enlists in the Marine Corps under a guaranteed tank contract. An inauspicious start that was quickly superseded by excelling in language study. Contract waived, a year at the Defense Language Institute to learn Russian and off to keep my ears on the big red machine during the Soviet years. Back to DLI for advanced Russian after reenlisting. Deploying. Then getting selected to get a commission. Earned a four-year degree in two years by majoring in Russian Language. It was a cop out, but I wanted to get back to the fleet. One summa cum laude graduation later, that's where I found myself. My first gig as a second lieutenant was on a general staff. I did well enough that I stayed at that level or higher for the rest of my career, while getting some choice side gigs – UAE, Bahrain, Korea, Russia, and Ukraine.

Major Martelle. I retired from the Marines after a couple years at the embassy in Moscow working arms control issues. The locals called me The German, because of my accent in Russian. That worked for me. It kept me off the radar. Just until it didn't. Expelled after two years for activities inconsistent with my diplomatic status, I went to Ukraine. Can't let twenty years of Russian language go to waste. More arms control. More diplomatic stuff. Then 9/11 and off to war. That was enough deployment for me. Then came retirement.

Department of Homeland Security was a phenomenally miserable gig. I quit that job quickly enough and went to law school. A second summa cum laude later and I was working for a high-end consulting firm performing business diagnostics, business law, and leadership coaching. More deployments. For the money they paid me, I was good with that. Just until I wasn't. Then I started writing. You'll find Easter eggs from my career hidden within all my books. Enjoy the stories.

Merri Maywether

Merri Maywether lives with her husband in rural Montana. You can find her in the town's only coffee house listening to three generations of Montanans share their stories. Otherwise, she's in the classroom or the school library, inspiring the next generation's writers.

Jenn Mitchell

Jenn Mitchell writes Urban Fantasy and Weird West, as well as culinary cozy mysteries under the pen name, J Lee Mitchell. She writes, cooks, and gardens in the heart of South Central Pennsylvania's Amish Country. When she's not doing these things, she dreams of training llama riding ninjas.

She enjoys traveling, quilting, hoarding cookbooks, Sanntangling, and spending time with the World's most patient and loving significant other.

Susan Odev

Susan has banked over three decades of work experience in the fields of personal and organizational development, being a freelance corporate trainer and consultant alongside holding down "real" jobs for over twenty-five years. Specializing in entrepreneurial mindsets, she has written several non-fiction business books, once gaining a coveted Amazon #1 best seller tag in business and entrepreneurship, an accolade she now strives to emulate with her fiction.

Currently working on her fifth novel, under a top secret pen name, the craft and marketing aspects of being a successful indie author equally fascinate and terrify her.

A lover of history with a criminal record collection, Susan lives in a retro orange and avocado world. Once described by a colleague as being an "onion," Susan has many layers, as have ogres (according to Shrek). She would like to think this makes her cool, her teenage children just think she's embarrassing.

PUBLISHERROCKET

FIND
PROFITABLE
KINDLE
KEYWORDS

Book Marketing Research
Made Simple!

writelink.to/pubrocket

MERCH FOR AUTHORS

Branded merch on Etsy, Amazon, and your own site.
Learn about extended stock licenses.
Includes sample contracts.

envato elements

Travel & Hotel Email Builder
By theemon

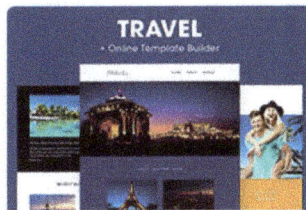

Travel Email Builder
By HyperPix

Kant - Email Template
By ThemeMountain

Olive - Fashion Email Template
By giantdesign

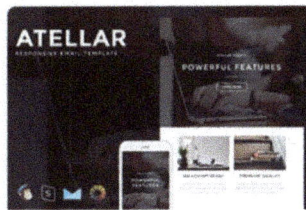

Metro App - Instapage Template
By Morad

ButaPest Email Template
By jeetuG

All the Email Templates you need and many other design elements, are available for a monthly subscription by subscribing to Envato Elements. The subscription costs $16.50 per month and gives you **unlimited access** to a massive and growing library of **1,500,000+** items that can be downloaded as often as you need (stock photos too)!

DOWNLOAD NOW

COME VISIT
the *Cake Machine* STAY for the *Conference.*

Las Vegas
Nevada
November
14-18, 2022

writelink.to/20Books

20 BOOKS TO 50K®
A RISING TIDE LIFTS ALL BOATS

www.ingramcontent.com/pod-product-compliance
Lightning Source LLC
Chambersburg PA
CBHW042340030426
42335CB00030B/3414